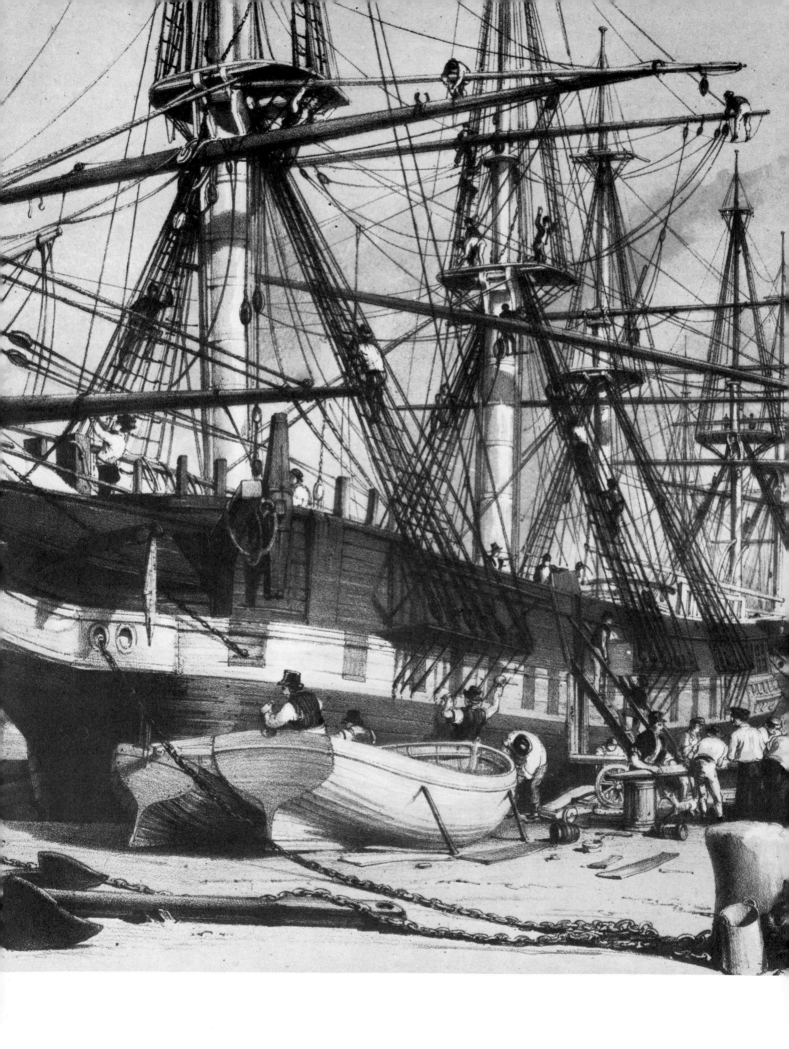

Michael Leitch

The romance of SAIL

Hamlyn
London · New York · Sydney · Toronto

Contents

Published by
The Hamlyn Publishing
Group Limited
London · New York ·
Sydney · Toronto
Astronaut House, Feltham,
Middlesex, England

© Copyright
The Hamlyn Publishing
Group Limited 1975
ISBN 0 600 37576 5

Printed in Hong Kong

previous spread
Ship maintenance at the West India Docks, London,
1830.

Captain Anson's *Centurion* blasts the Spanish
treasure ship *Nuestra Senora de Covadonga* in 1743;
from a painting by Samuel Scott.

Chapter 1
From Dugout to Full Rigger

top
One of the sea-going ships that made the voyage to Punt, *c.* 1480 BC.

above
Lateen-rigged gyassas on the Nile in recent times.

To fashion a boat, or a raft, by gouging a log or binding together a bundle of reeds – that is a first step. To launch this craft on water and see it float – that is another. To climb aboard and propel it by oar or paddle – that constitutes a still greater feat, the conquest of an element, water, through which man is not naturally adapted for travel (he may learn to swim, but usually can cope with short distances only). Then comes the grandest leap of all – to gather the power of another element, the wind, to drive the craft through the water.

The possibilities that unfurl in the mind when we pause to consider this concept, the *idea* of sailing, seem boundless; and in the ultra-superstitious world of early man such notions must have seemed especially outrageous to more than a few. The practicalities, too, have never been less than enough to daunt even the toughest of the nautical breed, whether they be Vikings creeping towards their dimly sensed New World, or the whisky-fired mate of a tea clipper, or the crew of an Iceland fishing boat committed for half a year to Arctic waters.

In fact, although sail was a great liberator – using it, men could travel faster and farther, carrying more people and goods than ever before – these advantages were to some extent balanced by the increased physical dangers confronting the sailor as he navigated ever greater spans of ocean, a servant kept in place by the machinations of his unpredictable master, the wind, and by the latter's moonstruck assistants, the tides.

Who were the first sailors? The documents that we know of form an incomplete picture; and doubtless some pioneering feats, carried out in remote corners, were never placed on record. But even if the documentary evidence were fuller, we might still do better to regard the discovery of sail as a kind of inspired revelation, something that was discovered many times over in places quite independent from each other, from China to Egypt to Peru.

The first clear records are Egyptian and tell of the river craft that traded on the Nile. There the natural conditions allowed a gentle beginning: the prevailing wind blew upstream and papyrus rafts made the journey propelled by paddles and a square-rigged sail; for

voyages downstream the current alone was sufficient, and the mast was taken down.

Sea-going craft followed, Egypt by her geographical position acting as a pivot to trade with the peoples of the Mediterranean and with those of the Red Sea and beyond. Wood, in the form of short planks of acacia, supplanted the reed as the favoured building material. Of special interest are the 'Punt' ships dispatched in about 1480 BC by Queen Hatshepsut along the east coast of Africa to carry spices and other goods to the land of Punt, now lost but thought to have

Model of an Egyptian ship, *c.* 2000 BC, steered by a single oar.

been in what is now Somalia. A rope running the length of each ship served to hold up its overhanging ends, which would otherwise have drooped owing to the vessel's length (some eighty feet overall). Fifteen oarsmen to each side ensured that steady progress could be maintained even on windless days; and the steering was by massive sweeps that swivelled from high posts mounted in the stern.

The First Traders

The Phoenicians of Tyre and Sidon were, with the Cretans, the great early masters of the Mediterranean sea trade. Rank upon rank of Lebanon's famous cedars was felled to supply a hungry ship-building industry. In *Ezekiel* XXVII there is an account of the citizens of Tyre, who 'have made all thy *ship* boards of fir trees of Senir: they have taken cedars from Lebanon to make masts for thee. *Of* the oaks of Bashan have they made thine oars; the company of the Ashurites have made thy benches *of* ivory, *brought* out of the isles of Chittim. Fine linen with broidered work from Egypt was that which thou spreadest forth to be thy sail.'

The Greeks distinguished two types of Phoenician ship – the *hippoi*, or horses, which were relatively slender fighting craft with a carved horse's head at the prow, and the *gauloi*, which were tub-like trading ancestors of the long-lived Mediterranean round ship. The Greeks themselves continued this pattern, refining their multi-oared galleys for greater speed and establishing the round merchantman as the staple trader on their tideless seas.

The merchant vessels of Rome reveal further progress: their architects added a triangular topsail to the main mast and introduced a smaller, square sail set on a mast sloping forward over the bows; this was called an *artemon*, and it added stability and made the ships easier to steer.

left
Egyptian river craft, *c.* 1450 BC; both means of propulsion, *i.e.* by oar and sail, are demonstrated.

bottom left
The Phoenician *hippos* or horse type, a narrow ship more suited to fighting than trade, *c.* 700 BC.

below
Model of a Roman trading ship of AD 200; steered by twin side rudders, she carries the artemon sail set forward over the bows.

The Vikings

In 1880 excavations in the blue clay at Gokstad, in Sweden, laid bare a remarkably well-preserved Viking merchant ship, since dated to around AD 900. She had been specially equipped with a burial chamber surmounted by a pitched roof, and sunk in the clay bearing the body of a dead warrior chieftain and a quantity of his personal belongings, among them his weapons, twelve horses and six dogs. Now heavily restored – and the ceremonial chamber removed – the Gokstad ship can be seen for what she was, a broad-beamed karv, a type of coastal trader, 79 feet long, 16½ feet in the beam, with a low gunwale amidships that curved steeply up at bow and stern.

A later discovery, of 1904, has added substantially to the store of knowledge about the Vikings and their ships. This was the Oseberg ship, built c. 800. Like the Gokstad ship, she was a coastal vessel propelled mostly by oars, though she carried a square-rigged sail made of homespun. Her bow was embellished with graceful carving. Together the two ships reveal several developments that set the Northern shipbuilders apart from their Mediterranean *confrères*. Firstly, the Vikings overlapped their hull planks clinker-style, whereas the Southern Europeans followed the carvel pattern of edge-to-edge building. Viking hulls were also reinforced by supplementary planks, and in design were double-ended – as opposed to the 'pear-drop' shape, broader in the stern, that was widely adopted in the Mediterranean. Another feature of the Viking ships is their high, sharp prow, needed to slice through the more turbulent waters of the North.

left
Swedish workmen at Gokstad dig out the Viking ship from its grave in the blue clay, 1880.

above
The Gokstad ship, partly restored and with the chieftain's burial chamber visible in the stern.

right
The broad-beamed Oseberg ship, excavated in 1904.

13

Medieval Round Ships

The merchant ships of medieval Europe were squat and businesslike, pot-bellied bugs that bobbled across the sea from one haven to the next. One type, known as the cog, was square-rigged with one or two masts, straight-ended and equipped with combinations of fore, after and top castles, which served as fighting platforms in times of danger. By now, too, the rudder had moved from the side of the ship and was mounted on the stern post.

The cog is particularly linked with the Hanseatic League, a North German association founded in the thirteenth century and centred on Lübeck, whose aim was to control trade in the Baltic by means of boycotting and through the formulation of its own maritime laws.

The League prospered for some three hundred years, about the time it took for shipbuilding to advance from stubby single-masters to the nobler concept of the full-rigged ship.

Further south, ships were more slender and the fore-and-aft lateen rig was favoured. This made use of a large sail in the shape of a right-angled triangle that was attached along its hypotenuse to a long sloping yard. The lateen rig, which made it easier to sail against the wind, was to reach its high point in the three-masted caravels that worked the coasts of Portugal and the Mediterranean in the fourteenth and fifteenth centuries.

A cog, depicted on the Seal of Stralsund, 1329; note the position of the rudder, now moved from the side and mounted on the stern post.

Marco Polo's expedition arrives at Carcan, after leaving Venice in 1271.

top
Model of a lateen-rigged merchantman, based on a
relief from Milan dated 1339.

above
Model of an English Cinque Ports ship of the thirteenth
century.

The Carrack

After the doughty but limited cog came the carrack, a grander design fitted for trade, battle or both. The carrack had two or more square-rigged masts and a further mast, the mizzen, which carried a three-cornered lateen sail and was placed aft of the main mast. The latter's function was to improve the steering qualities of an otherwise square-rigged and therefore at times cumbersome vessel.

Further developments were at hand: a ship from Northern Europe was depicted with a spritsail, an auxiliary sail that could be set beneath the bowsprit; while a picture from Venice showed yet another mast stepped aft of the mizzen and carrying a lateen sail. This was known as the bonaventure. Decking, too, had become more elaborate, and the sheer, or fore-and-aft curvature, was increasingly pronounced. By now the sixteenth century had dawned, and the glorious complexities of the galleon and other 'great ships' were flitting through the dreams of naval architects in Spain and in Northern Europe; fruition would not be long delayed.

left
Model of a Flemish *kraek* or carrack, *c.* 1470, having two square-rigged masts and a lateen-rigged mizzen. Supports are shown for awnings on both fore and after castles; from the latter jut the barrels of four cannon.

top
It was customary to punish mutineers by ducking them or by transfixing or lashing them to the mast; from a woodcut in Olaus Magnus's *History of the Northern Peoples*, 1555.

right
A carrack with a commodious after castle; from an illustration in Breydenbach's *Voyage to the Holy Land*, 1486.

Chapter 2

Early Fighting Ships

The warships of the ancient world led with their beaks – sharp bronze ramming devices fitted to the bows, at their best when smashed against the side of an enemy galley, holing it below the water line and sending its company to make their peace with the gods of the deep. To achieve such spectacular results, many factors were called into play, but above all others came the necessity for speed. The typical Mediterranean war galley was long, low and slender, and essentially oar-powered for maximum speed-plus-control at a time when the art of sailing still contained many mysteries. A square-rigged sail was carried, but its purpose was auxiliary to that of the oarsmen, who might be double- or even treble-banked with outriggers supporting, usually, the outermost bank of oars.

The Phoenicians of the seventh century BC favoured the bireme, a galley propelled by two banks of oarsmen, as their principal warship. After them the Greeks worked to perfect the trireme, in which, in the view of Björn Landström, the Swedish authority, the oars lay at three levels or in groups of three. During battle, leather tarpaulins were lowered along each side to protect the oarsmen. Overall these craft, rowed by some 170 men, measured approximately 120 feet in length and 18 feet in the beam. The mainmast was lowered before battle. The Romans also built triremes, and the oared galley type persisted until well into the Middle Ages and then in dwindling numbers up to the end of the seventeenth century.

Lacking gunpowder, the early fleet commanders relied on archers and men-at-arms fighting at close quarters to win the day. A sea fight between two galleys was a kind of two-way siege, the object being to board and then overpower one's opponent. The fighting men went into battle stationed on a central platform running the length of the galley; once this had fallen, the fight was as good as over. At the Battle of Salamis (480 BC), in which the mainland Greeks defeated a mixed fleet under the ultimate command of Xerxes, King of Persia, we know that each Athenian

Model of a Phoenician bireme with central fighting platform, seventh century BC.

trireme carried a boarding party of 18, of which 14 were javelin-armed hoplites and four were bowmen. Some of the enemy ships had a greater deck area and could hold up to 40 fighting men – though at the expense of speed and manoeuvrability. On the day the Greek squadrons were faster and more decisive; the poet Aeschylus, in *The Persians*, describes thus the beginnings of the rout that followed:

At first the Persian line withstood this shock; but soon
Our crowding vessels choked the channel, and none
Could help each other; soon their armoured prows
Smashed inward on their allies, and broke off short
The banks of oars, while the Greek ships skilfully
Encircled and attacked them from all sides.

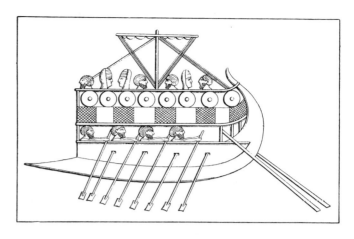

left
Greek merchantman and war galley of the fifth century
BC, depicted on the side of an amphora.

above
Assyrian war galley, *c.* 700 BC.

below
Model of a Greek galley; this view is of the port quarter.

Byzantine Firepower

After the collapse of Rome the most enterprising warriors in the Mediterranean were the Byzantines. They were ruled from Constantinople (Istanbul) by a succession of dynasties until their capital was finally overrun by the Turks in 1453. For more than a thousand years they preserved the classical traditions that had run to seed in Greece and Rome, while their powerful armed forces buttressed Western Europe against barbarian attacks. In particular, the Byzantines needed a strong fleet to patrol and keep open their many trade routes in the Mediterranean.

During that period naval strategy advanced but little, remaining centred on the swift and manoeuvrable oar-powered galley. Nevertheless, by the sixth century a new type of galley had entered service, the dromon, from the Greek word *dromos*, meaning runner. This placed greater reliance on sail, each vessel carrying up to three lateen-rigged sails in addition to a double bank of oars on each side, manned by 150–200 men.

The dromon was a heavy warship and was armed accordingly, with missile-throwing engines and a menacing type of flamethrower. *Ballistae*, heavy crossbows, rained javelins on enemy fleets, and on occasion a version of the siege catapult was used, launching stone balls from a cup-shaped holder. The presence of such weapons indicates a move away from the kind of naval battle that was fought uniquely at close quarters and towards a two-part strategy in which the artillery first softened up the adversary, who was then finished off by ramming, with or without the assistance of a boarding party.

Perhaps the most advanced weapon of the day was Greek fire. This was used at close range and was launched from a bronze tube mounted in the bows; an inflammable liquid was pumped through the tube by means of a plunger and ignited on impact with water. Projected onto and around the wooden hulls of a hostile fleet, Greek fire was destructive of both morale and ships.

below
Model of a Byzantine dromon, sixth century AD.

opposite top
Greek fire; projected through a bronze tube, it ignited as soon as it touched water.

opposite bottom
A land *ballista*; modified versions of this giant crossbow were carried in dromons and used to bombard the enemy with heavy javelins.

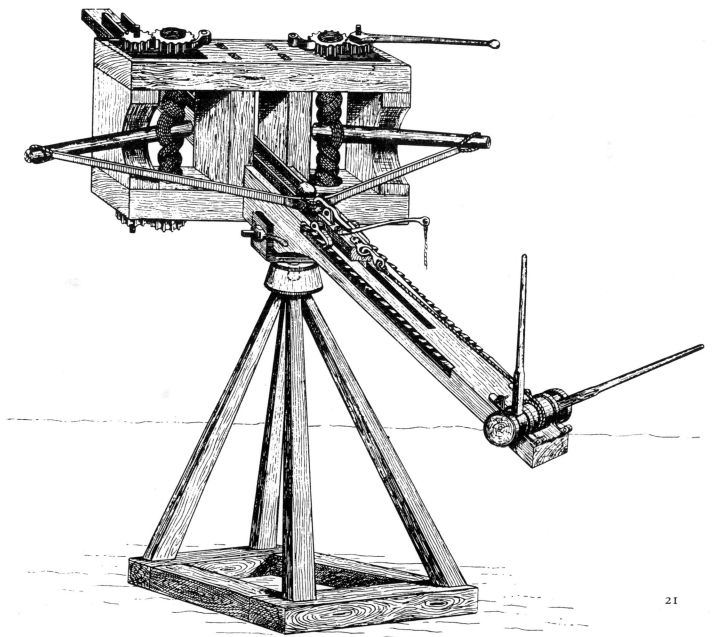

Longships and Roundships

The late eleventh-century Bayeux Tapestry measures more than 230 feet long and 19 inches wide and traces in 79 scenes the story of the Norman Conquest and the events that came immediately before it. As a visual document of the warships of the day it is of inestimable value: it clearly shows how the invading Normans ferried men, horses and supplies across the English Channel in a fleet of Viking-style longships driven by a single square-rigged sail and steered by a sweep mounted to starboard. (The term star- or steer-board gave rise to the nautical term for the right side, since the steering oar was always mounted on that side; ships in those days docked with the left side next to the port in order not to damage the steering oar, hence the companion term port, meaning left side.)

By the time of the Hundred Years' War (1337–1453), vessels of war had become rounder and carried fore, after and top castles from which archers and men-at-arms launched their attacks. We have already seen in the evolution of the carrack (pages 16–17) how ships became more elaborate; now again we can see this process applied to the fighting ship. Although the oared galley was by no means dead yet, the number of masts on sailing ships had increased to three or four; in this way the fast sailing ship was beginning to make the challenge that would eventually bring about the eclipse of the oar-driven warship. Another feature of interest in the new sailing ships concerns the growth of the after castle: once a rudely tacked-on fighting platform, it steadily became more capacious and was incorporated into the design of the hull itself.

below
Norman longships transport men and horses across the English Channel for the invasion of 1066; from the Bayeux Tapestry.

opposite top
The bow and the sword were still the main weapons of the offensive in 1372, when the Castilian fleet attacked the Earl of Pembroke's men off La Rochelle.

opposite bottom
Three-masted ships with imposing fore and after castles formed the bulk of the Duc de Bourbon's fleet on this expedition to Barbary, c. 1470; in the foreground is a typical, if overloaded, Mediterranean galley.

Tubs of War

On these pages are three versions of warships depicted by fifteenth-century artists. The two paintings (as distinct from the line drawing) purport to show scenes from the Crusades: the dockside picture records the taking of Damietta in 1249, and the other is of Christian ships, mostly at anchor, in the Bosphorus before an assault that took place in 1204.

In both works, however, the artists have evidently taken near-contemporary ships for their models, and consequently are some two hundred years out of date. In addition, the Damietta artist has furnished the castles of his vessels with some quaint roofs that recall more the mansards of Paris than part of a thirteenth- or

even fifteenth-century troopship. The Bosphorus illustration is more accurate in its fashion, with several features that are interesting from a nautical point of view. Among these are the tall stout masts, composed of a number of spars lashed together; the ropes are clearly shown at intervals on each of the masts. The fore castles taper almost to a point, and reaching beyond them are hooks designed to tear at enemy rigging. These ships were clinker-built, and their hulls were reinforced with vertical battens.

The line drawing is a curiosity that may owe more to artist's whim than reality. Taken from an historical work published in 1472, it shows a kind of oar-driven,

heavily castellated washtub crammed with full-armed soldiers firing in every direction. Perhaps we should concentrate our attention on the picture's heraldic arrangement and pass over the details. One item, though, has a special significance: three of the men are using handguns.' These were a comparatively recent innovation, and possibly appeared for the first time on a battlefield at Crécy in 1346. From that time onward, the gun was to have a profound influence not only on the weapons used in naval warfare but also on the ships that carried them.

The Turbulent Mediterranean Sea

Naval history has now passed into the Gunpowder Age. For the next two hundred years strategists and artillerymen strove to find the best possible ways of blending gun and ship. During that time the galley retained much of its centuries-old standing as a manoeuvrable and basically reliable gun platform – if a limited one in terms of the weight of cannon which any one galley could support. It was, furthermore, becoming ever clearer that sail, with its promise of greater speed, was a more desirable means of propulsion if battles were to be fought, in part anyway, at a distance.

The period from 1470 to the 1570s saw the emergence on the one hand of the gunned carrack, forerunner of the Spanish Armada ships. This type was built by nations with an Atlantic or northern seaboard. On the other hand, in the Mediterranean, where winds were lighter, the galley reached new peaks of refinement: it was armed with long-barrelled cannon mounted on the foredeck, and propelled by fewer oars manned by more men, up to five per oar. The galley's inherent limitations were nonetheless recognized, and it was to some degree superseded by a compromise type, the galleass. This new type carried oars and one or more lateen sails, and was the result of efforts to add extra speed and weight, while at the same time preserving the galley's independence of movement, provided by her oars.

left
Warships at the Siege of Constantinople; from de la Brocquière's *Voyage d'Outremer*, published in 1455.

top right
War galleys and carracks before Tunis, 1535; from a contemporary German print.

bottom right
The handguns and cannon of Christian and Turk spit flame and smoke at Lepanto, 1571.

27

Oars plus Sails – the Climax

The Battle of Lepanto, fought in 1571 between the Turks and the Christians, marked the high point, in terms of numbers present and blood spilt, in the careers of both galley and galleass. Yet for all the impact of the Christians' galleasses, whose long-range cannon caused heavy damage to the Turkish fleet before the latter could close to within range of their own guns, these ships represented an outmoded form of warfare. The future undoubtedly lay with the heavier broadsides that the full-rigged ship could level at an adversary.

For a considerable time, however, the galley/galleass persisted in Mediterranean waters; even at the end of the seventeenth century the French were still building a variant, the réale, to protect their interests in the region. These vessels were some 150 feet long, 20 feet in the beam, and were propelled by 427 oarsmen, seated seven to an oar, and by two large lateen sails that were furled before battle. The latter tactic, however much more freedom of movement it gave to those on board, made the réale slow on the turn and conspicuously vulnerable to the fast sailing ship in anything stronger than calm weather. At such times a single broadside might suffice to blast the unfortunate réale from view, and in due time this type, along with the galley, was phased out of the various navies flanking the Mediterranean.

Model of a French réale, a type that persisted up to the end of the seventeenth century.

opposite top
Oars and masts flail together in the chaos of Lepanto, where galley and galleass performed the last of their grand set-pieces.

opposite bottom
Corsair galleys in the Mediterranean.

29

Chapter 3
Traders and Explorers

The growing hunger for knowledge engendered by the Renaissance movement in Western Europe provoked a strong desire in men's minds to expand the physical boundaries of the known world. By seeing more, they hoped both to learn more and to enrich the store of what they already knew.

These needs began to manifest themselves some years before shipbuilding reached the next logical climax in its progress, the era of the 'great ships'. For the explorers, however, reliable and adequate ships already existed in the shape of the sturdy carrack and the caravel. They had little need of vast ships manned by hundreds of men, as we can well see if we look at the numbers of officers and men who in 1492 crossed the Atlantic with Columbus. The total for all three ships in that tiny fleet was 87 – 39 on the flagship *Santa Maria*, 26 on board the *Pinta* and 22 on the *Nina*. These modest figures – fewer per ship than went on Queen Hatshepsut's expedition to Punt three thousand years earlier – also underline a basic difference between the limited aims of oar-powered craft, continually dependent on human leverage to propel them, and the more or less infinite possibilities that sail had by then placed within men's reach.

A tapestry showing the departure of Columbus's fleet in 1492; all three ships are shown as square-rigged, whereas it is more likely that one of them, the *Nina*, set out with a lateen rig and was later converted and given a square sail on her fore- and mainmasts.

Perils from the sea — in the shape of flying fish
dive-bombing the deck, also albacores and strange,
plump, shark-like creatures.

Carrack or Caravel?

Over the centuries authors have with variable accuracy designated ships as being of this or that type, and shipbuilders have compounded the confusion by, quite rightly, designing and adapting according to principles of need rather than of slavish imitation. As a result few ships are entirely alike, and group names can mislead.

Two of the most difficult types to separate are the carrack and the caravel. Although, for example, most of what we would now class as caravels were lateen-rigged throughout, a disconcertingly large number has been recorded of other so-called caravels that had one or more square-rigged sails. Certain ambiguities no doubt arise at source, from the original Portuguese word *caravela*, used in the thirteenth century as a vaguely generic term for fishing boats. In time caravels became associated with the lateen rig, but towards the end of the fifteenth century, as Björn Landström states in his book *Sailing Ships*, caravels were 'often fitted, in Spain at least, with the usual ship's rigging, with a square foresail and mainsail and a lateen mizzen'.

At that time, too, Columbus was writing of his hopes of acquiring 'three or four well-equipped caravels' for his trans-Atlantic voyage. In the event, though, his fleet appears to have consisted of two carracks – square-rigged on fore and mainmast and with a lateen sail on the mizzen – and one lateen-rigged caravel, the *Nina*. The latter was then, it seems, converted on the voyage, during a four-week stay in the Canary Islands, and re-equipped with a rig similar to that of the other ships.

left
Model of a traditional lateen-rigged caravel.

Model of the *Pinta*, in appearance an ordinary carrack
but referred to in her day as a caravel.

Vasco da Gama

From among the rush of explorers quitting Europe for far-off places, it is interesting to look for a moment at the greatest achievement of one of them, Vasco da Gama (c. 1469–1524). The discoveries of this Portuguese navigator are of special importance since it was his voyage to India that paved the way for Portugal's

previous page
The city and port of Seville, alive with a mixed assemblage of galleys, galleasses, carracks and small craft; from a sixteenth-century painting by Sanchez Cuello.

conquest of the East Indies and the setting-up of an enduring east-west trade.

He set sail from Lisbon on 8 July 1497 with four vessels, rounded the Cape of Good Hope and reached Malindi on the east coast of Africa. From there he sailed directly across the Indian Ocean, arriving at Calicut on 19 May 1498 having completed the first voyage from Western Europe around Africa to the East. It is said of that voyage that the goods da Gama took home from India paid a return of 6,000 per cent – a statistic which must have brought saliva to the lips of merchants from Lisbon to Stockholm once the news had circulated. Trade with the Indies was about to become big business (though profits were never to match da Gama's reputed figure).

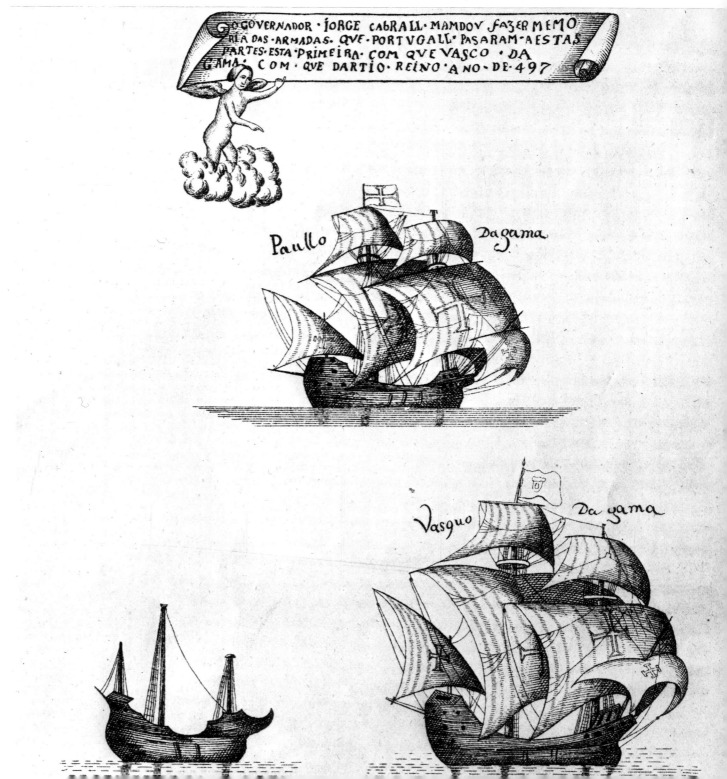

VASCO DE GAMA

left
The ships of da Gama's first expedition, which set out
from Lisbon in July 1497.

Vasco da Gama (*c.* 1469–1524), the Portuguese
explorer commissioned by King Emanuel I to make a
journey by sea to India.

The Mapmakers

The explorers of the fifteenth and sixteenth centuries can with some justice be called the true begetters of the atlas industry. Following in their wake, and working from their reports of how the world looked beyond the horizon, a succession of cartographers set about founding the business of producing and publishing maps, atlases and globes, a business that has swelled from an inaugural trickle to become, in our own times, a regular inundation.

Among the earliest of the great cartographers was Gerard Mercator (1512–94). Born in Rupelmonde, near Antwerp, he specialized until he was 40 in making mathematical and astronomical instruments; he also produced a number of remarkable globes and published his first map in 1537. Later he completed a three-part atlas that was published between 1585 and 1595. After his death, the distribution of his maps remained a family business until 1606, when the Flemish cartographer and engraver Jodocus Hondius acquired the plates. Hondius, perhaps best known for his work as a globemaker and for his illustrations to the voyages of Drake and Cavendish, continued to publish the Mercator maps until his own death in 1611. In our illustration the two men are portrayed side by side in a kind of architectural cartouche similar to those used to frame the titles of maps and charts.

right
A map of Florida and the West Indies; from an atlas by Lazaro Luis, 1563.

opposite top
The sixteenth-century cartographers Gerard Mercator, left, and Jodocus Hondius.

opposite bottom
A cosmographer in his study, after Stradanus; the room is dominated by a large model carrack suspended from the ceiling.

GERARDUS MERCATOR NATUS
RUPELMUNDÆ III NON.MARTII ANNO
CIƆIƆXII:VIXIT ANN.LXXXII.M.VIII.D.
XXVI:DENATUS IV NON.DECEMBRIS
ANNO CIƆIƆXCIV.

IUDOCUS HONDIUS NATUS IN
PAGO FLANDRIÆ DICTO WACKENE XVI
KALEND.NOVEMBRIS ANNO CIƆIƆLXIII:
VIXIT ANN.XLVII.M.VII.D.XXIX:DENAT:
US XIV KAL.MARTII ANNO CIƆIƆCXII.

Ioan.Stradanus invent.   Phls Galle excud.

Bruegel's Galleons

After the carrack and the caravel came the age of the great ships and the galleons. Ships of the latter type usually had four masts and were slimmer than the carracks, with a smaller fore castle built within the bows and a projecting beak. Björn Landström has suggested that it was the latter's resemblance to the ram carried on the galleys that occasioned the name galleon.

These ships were heavily armed and were intended for war rather than trade. They are nevertheless included at this juncture, in a relatively peaceful chapter, in order to show how shipbuilding progressed in the period between the heavy carracks of the fifteenth century and the long-distance merchantmen that from the late sixteenth century began to venture between Europe and the Indies.

Several engravings by Frans Huys after Pieter Bruegel the Elder (1525–69) depict galleons as the artist would have seen them in the 1560s or thereabouts. Bruegel's strong line lends added force to the ships' towering masts and rigging, on which insect-like crew members scramble to and fro, and to the awesome billowing of sails caught by the wind.

opposite top
A galleon and a lateen-rigged galley.

opposite bottom
Galleon leaving harbour, 1565.

above
A sixteenth-century warship; at top right Icarus, the
legendary flyer, makes a surprise appearance.

41

East Indiamen

Trade with the East Indies grew steadily during the sixteenth century and was then placed on a firmer footing in the early 1600s with the founding of the British and Dutch East India Companies. 'Pepper and spice/ And all things nice' were, in the words of the old rhyme, what the public in Europe craved, for with such aromatic additives their rotting meat dishes could be made tolerable and their puddings, not to mention their tempers, sweetened.

The early East Indiamen were built on galleon lines, with a spritsail and topsails carried on three masts; in time a third sail, the topgallant, was added to the fore and mainmasts. From the beginning of the eighteenth century most East Indiamen were classified as frigates. Armament was heavy, as it had to be when the chief trading nations – England, Holland, France and Spain – were forever at each other's throats; company ships attacked their rivals with much the same vigour that was needed for the complex political and business deals which the company men struck with their willing and not-so-willing Eastern associates.

right
Merchant ships at the East India Company's yard, Deptford; from a painting by Isaac Sailmaker, 1721.

below
Detail from a map showing a sixteenth-century merchantman in the East Indies.

below right
Another eighteenth-century view of the Thames near Deptford, by Samuel Scott; the dockyard was closed at the end of the century.

CEANE DE LINDE ORIENTALE

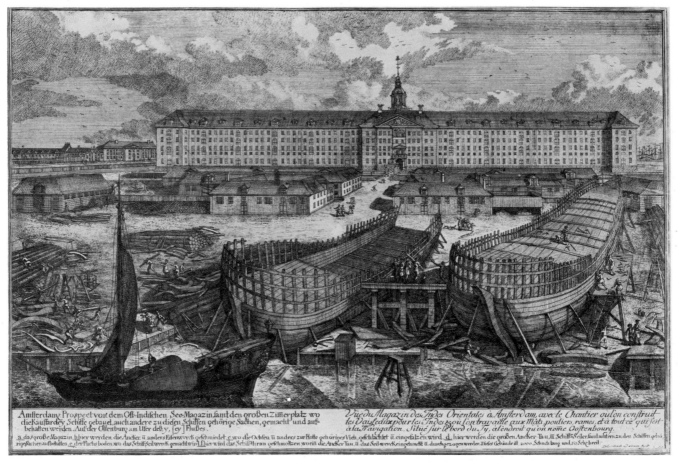

Amsterdams Prospect von dem Ost-Indischen See-Magazin samt den großen Zimerplatz wo die Kauffardey Schiffe gebauet, auch andere zu diesen Schiffen gehörige Sachen, gemacht und auf behalten werden. Auf der Oftenburg am Ufer dez y, [ey] Flußes.

Vue du Magazin des Indes Orientales à Amsterdam, avec le Chantier ou l'on construit les Vaisseaux pour les Indes: ou l'on travaille aux Mâts, poutiers, rames, & à tout ce qui sert à la Navigation. Situé sur le bord du Iy, à l'endroit qu'on nomme Oostenbourg.

The Amsterdam shipyard of the Dutch East India Company, by J. A. Delsenbach, 1733.

A mariner's telescope of 1661, shown extended and with the lens covers detached.

The East Indiaman *Neptune* seen in 1776 fitted with a replacement device after she had lost her rudder at sea.

45

Small Traders

By the seventeenth century numerous trading ships of relatively modest proportions were to be found at work off the coasts of Europe. One of the most common types was the fluyt, a round-sterned vessel of Dutch origin. Another was the pinnace, a small-scale full-rigged ship with a flat stern that in its double-decked version resembled the frigate; the latter type began the century as a small, swift man o' war, then grew rapidly into a formidable full-rigged warship carrying sixty or more guns. All three types belonged to a group noted by Fredrik af Chapman, the eighteenth-century Swedish shipwright, as having beakheads. Other members of the group were the hagboat and the pink. Another group consisted of blunt-bowed types, and included the cat and the barque.

Differences between the various types were on the whole small: Chapman distinguished his types purely on hull design and regardless of rig, whereas others named their types after particular rigs. The latter system makes for swifter recognition, since sails, their numbers and arrangement are more easily spotted at a distance than minor hull details; and in time this system was generally adopted.

above
A Dutch fluyt off Rotterdam; from a grisaille by Abraham van Salm, *c.* 1710.

below
Dutch ships salute Peter the Great during his visit to Amsterdam in 1698; from a painting by Abraham Storck.

right
The flattened bows of a Danish timber barque; from a painting by Samuel Scott.

Mediterranean Traditional

On these pages can be seen the gaff-rigged mainsail, supported by a diagonal spar or sprit, that was an important feature of many traditional sailing craft of the Mediterranean. The odd man out is the Spanish felucca, a two-masted, lateen-rigged ship whose design seems to pay tribute to the speedy, yacht-like chebek, used in the seventeenth century by the Algerian Corsairs on their sorties of terror and pillage. The felucca was nonetheless a cargo ship, long in the bow-sprit and transom-sterned, with her mainmast raked some way forward – though not so steeply as that of the Greek sacoleva, also shown.

right
Model of a Spanish felucca.

below
Constructional details and sail plan of a Greek sacoleva.

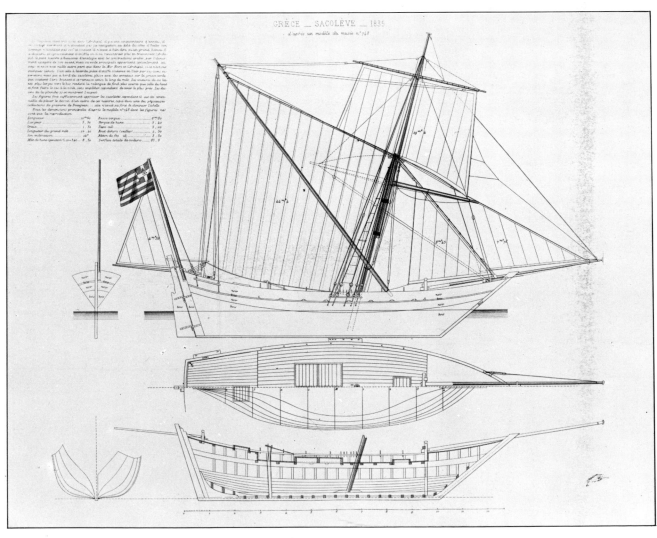

A Turkish sloop in detail, together with smaller sketches of other craft found in the region of Constantinople.

Captain Cook

Captain James Cook (1728–79), described by a contemporary as 'the most able and enlightened navigator that England ever produced', made three great voyages. On the first, he surveyed New Zealand and discovered and surveyed the east coast of Australia. This voyage, which lasted from 1768–71, was made in the barque HMS *Endeavour*, formerly the Whitby collier *Earl of Pembroke*, a sturdy and roomy vessel that was also of shallow draught – a great asset when operating off unknown coasts. She could, furthermore, be put aground in tidal waters for repair work; this was something that could not have been done with a larger or more sharp-featured vessel.

On the second voyage (1772–75) Cook thoroughly explored the South Pacific, proving that a Great Southern Continent did not exist. His ships were the *Resolution* and the *Adventure*. The former also accompanied Cook on his third voyage (1776–80), together with the *Discovery*, when he discovered Hawaii, surveyed three thousand miles of the west coast of North America and penetrated the Bering Strait into the Arctic. Cook himself did not return from this voyage; he was killed by natives in Hawaii during a skirmish. The eminence of their victim did not go unregarded. Cook's body was divided ceremonially and burned, and his bones were scraped in the funeral rites reserved for a chief or god.

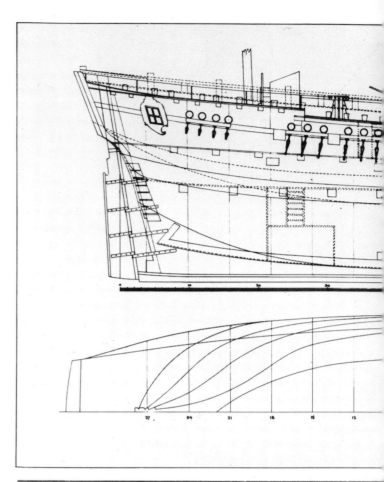

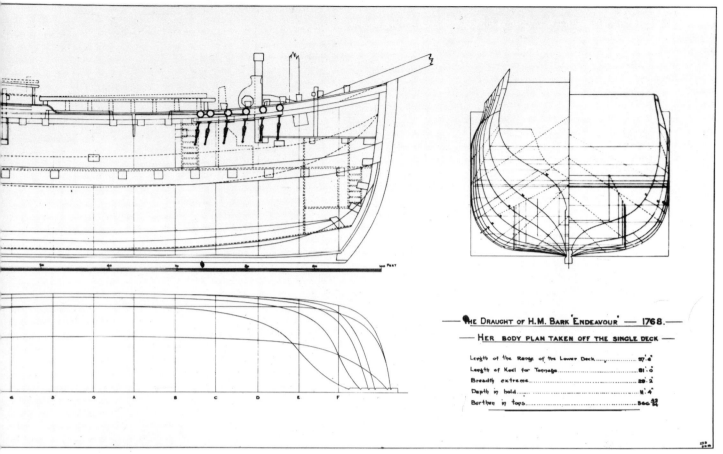

above
Plans of HMS *Endeavour*, showing the almost flat bottom on which she could be stood for repairs without undue risk – an invaluable asset thousands of miles from the nearest dry dock.

far left
Captain James Cook (1728–79).

left
On the second voyage, the *Resolution* and *Adventure* are shown in Tahiti; from a painting by William Hodges, official artist to the voyage.

The Whaling Trade

'A dead whale or a stove boat' – this line from the whaleman's song was a tough maxim to live by; but many did and many of these were rewarded for their work with an icy grave. The fight with the whale had to be carried out from an open rowing boat; only by getting really close could the hunters lodge their harpoons to good effect. If the angered whale then rolled on the boat, the results can easily be imagined.

The whalers worked mostly in the chill waters of the extreme north and south; at times they might be away from their home port for as long as five years. The conditions of life aboard are well caught in a passage in *Ships and Men*, by W. J. Bassett-Lowke and George Holland:

'The whale-ship was stout and slow, blunt in the bows and square in the stern, and for size was counted a big ship, though by no means comparable to an East Indiaman. She had no rake to her three masts, her deck was flush, and she carried little sail. Every inch of her space was designed for carrying. In an American whaler the ship's food-stores were packed in casks, which when empty could be filled with oil. Her bulwarks were fitted with heavy wooden davits for lowering the whale-boats, and the boats were carried under them; indeed, she seemed full of boats, for these were stowed in every odd corner of the ship. Up aloft on the mastheads was the crow's nest, an open platform, not a steel cabin with a telephone as on a modern whaler, but a perch just big enough for the look-out

above
A massive slaughter of whales and seals in Arctic waters.

opposite top
Natives grapple with whales off the coast of Zanzibar.

opposite bottom
The larboard boat of the *Ann Alexander*, an American whaler, is savaged by a sperm whale in the South Pacific.

man to stand on while watching for sight of a whale, and a ring of iron, through which he squeezed his body and on which he could rest his arms, as his only security. In many whaling centres a barrel was used. Perilously he stood, like a figure on a monument, gazing over the seas till his watch was done. The whaler carried usually a crew of forty or fifty men, including the ship-master, surgeon, carpenters, and coopers. . . . It was a dangerous calling and their crews included 'hoodlums' without experience. . . . There are many records of ships being sunk by fighting whales. Melville's *Pequod* has been lost again and again in fact. The tale of the *Essex* lost in the South Pacific in 1819 is one of the most terrible of all – of men a thousand miles from land, of appalling sufferings from hunger and thirst, of cannibalism among the mad crew, and, at last, rescue for the remaining few.'

Chapter 4
The Gunned Sailing Ship

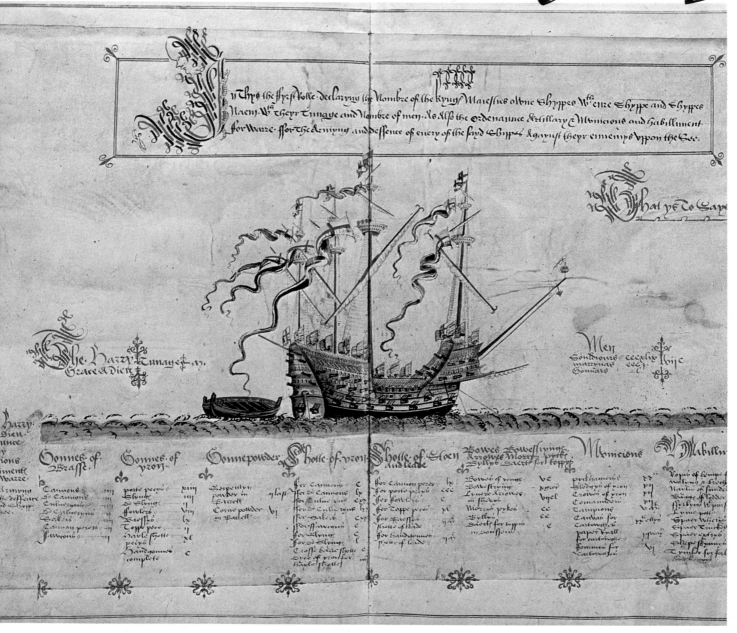

The *Henry Grâce à Dieu* or *Great Harry*, depicted in
the Rolls of Anthony Anthony, 1546.

The four-masted *Henry Grâce à Dieu*, or *Great Harry*, was one of the first of the 'great ships'. These massive vessels came to symbolize the high aspirations in the sixteenth century of the great maritime powers, eager not only to explore, expand, conquer, and grow rich on the proceeds, but concerned also that other nations should *see* and in some measure feel overshadowed by their new wealth and power. These ships also established the gunned sailing ship as the fighting vessel of the future, able to outstrip and outgun the galley/galleass types in almost any conditions.

Since its first appearance on the battlefield in the mid-fourteenth century, the gun had grown both in size and hitting power. For the maritime powers of Northern Europe the implications could not be ignored: henceforth sea power would turn around the ships armed with the most powerful guns, capable in theory of pounding their rivals out of the water while they themselves remained out of range.

When the *Great Harry* was built for King Henry VIII in 1514, all these manifestations of the Renaissance

Warships of the sixteenth century, mostly carracks and galleys, are shown off Naples; from a painting by Pieter Bruegel the Elder.

spirit – the urgent desire for economic growth allied to scientific progress in such appropriate fields as shipbuilding, navigation and gunnery – could not be expected suddenly to produce an immaculate new ship type. In the case of the *Great Harry*, the firepower of her 184 guns – a very large quantity for her time – was achieved at a considerable sacrifice to mobility. Between 1536 and 1539 she received a substantial refit; even so, despite her mass of topsails and topgallants, she still resembled a floating fortress rather than a mobile man of war. In her, though, we can clearly see the principles that would dictate the pattern of future battles at sea. These would be resolved largely through exchanges of broadsides delivered by lines of heavy guns firing through ports cut in the hull sides of powerful ships carrying a mass of sail.

Two sixteenth-century Spanish falconets; these light breech-loading pieces were fixed to swivel mounts.

55

above

The *Prince Royal* at Flushing; from a painting by Hendrik Vroom. Built in 1610 by Phineas Pett, shipbuilder to King James I of England, she had three gun decks with 56 guns, and at 210 feet overall was the largest ship of her time.

left

A heavy four-masted ship of the galleon type, built in Amsterdam; from a drawing by Willem Barents, 1594.

right

Men of war in Calais Roads, 1545.

Defeat of the Armada

The *Ark Royal*, Lord Howard's flagship in the battle.
right
A stylized version of the defeat of the Spanish Armada, from a design for a tapestry commissioned to celebrate the event.

Only 17 years after Lepanto, the focus of sea power having shifted westward to the Atlantic nations, the naval forces of England and Spain met in the English Channel for the first major confrontation between gunned sailing ships. The English fleet was outnumbered. Thirty-four royal warships and a quantity of armed merchantmen faced an Armada consisting of 65 galleons supported by some 50 smaller ships, four galleasses and four galleys. In terms of men the English had about 15,000, the Spanish twice that number.

As the Armada advanced up the Channel it was pursued and harried by the English operating at long range; but the invasion fleet stayed together and anchored safely in Calais Roads. There, it was planned, the Duke of Parma would shortly arrive with a second fleet. This failed to happen. Parma was pinned down in the Netherlands by Dutch rebels, and, as the Armada waited, the English sent in their fire-ships on the night tide. Such was their effectiveness – augmented by the universal fear of fire at sea in wooden ships – that the great Spanish fleet was eviscerated in a matter of

hours. The survivors broke and fled, some being forced to return home past the north of Scotland.

Judged as a duel between gunned fighting ships, the affair of the Armada was a great anti-climax. Yet the form it took was not untypical of other large-scale confrontations: the weaker side, the English, kept a shrewd distance until the moment came to operate their master-stroke. Because of their caution, such bombardments as they levelled at the Spanish in the early stages had almost no effect. On the other side the Spanish, though stronger, were caught out while waiting for reinforcements which they hoped would guarantee their eventual supremacy. In brief, this was a fight in which neither side wished to be committed until the moment was exactly right. Such respect for timing, while not exactly new, was no doubt reinforced by the daunting presence of massed cannon on either side; still largely an unknown factor, the guns inspired a special kind of awe.

The Raising of the *Vasa*

A reconstruction by I. N. Kowarsky of the Swedish
ship *Vasa* as she may have looked in her brief active
life.

The *Vasa*, Sweden's great ship, heeled over and sank within sight of the thousands of well-wishers gathered to cheer the start of her maiden voyage. That was in 1628, and for more than three centuries she lay on the bottom of the sea, until in 1956 she was found and five years later brought to the surface and towed into dry dock. Now she is as valuable a maritime museum piece as could be hoped for – a carefully restored, 1,300-ton prestige ship, 170 feet long, 35 feet in the beam, but of perhaps perilously shallow draught at barely 14 feet. This, added to the unusually great weight she carried above the water-line, may explain why the mighty *Vasa* tipped over in her first squall.

right
The lower gun deck after the mud of centuries had been scooped away; these gun carriages were all built for 24-pounders.

below
The *Vasa* stands in the dry dock to which she was towed in 1961.

Gingerbread Days

'Gingerbread' is a popular term for the gilded carving lavished on the sterns and hull sides of many a fighting ship. This practice reached its greatest heights of ornateness in the late seventeenth century. Some years before that climax, in 1637, one Thomas Heywood described with unsparing, if appropriate, preciosity the astonishing frills that were heaped on the *Sovereign of the Seas*, a prestige ship designed by Phineas Pett for Charles I.

'I begin at the Beak-head,' he began, 'where I desire you to take notice, that upon the stemme-head there is a Cupid, or a Child resembling him, bestriding, and bridling a Lyon, which importeth, that sufferance may curbe Insolence, and Innocence restraine violence; which alludeth to the great mercy of the King, whose Type is a proper Embleme of that great Majesty, whose Mercy is above all his Workes.'

Mr Heywood's verbal caress continues along the length of the great ship, and then:

'I come now to the Stearne, where you may perceive upon the upright of the upper Counter, standeth Victory. . . . Her wings are equally display'd; on one

Arme she weareth a Crowne, on the other a Laurell, which imply Riches and Honour. . . . In the lower Counter of the Sterne, on either side of the Helme is this Inscription,

He who Seas, Windes, and Navies doth protect, Great Charles, thy great Ship in her course direct.'

The French, too, as might be expected, shared this taste for extravagant ship decoration, and practised it well into the eighteenth century. In England, though, the cult of gingerbread became gradually modified; the amount of carving was reduced and gilt was then reserved for the royal arms only, the rest being carried out in yellow paint.

far left
Gingerbread view of the *Sovereign of the Seas*; this remarkable piece of floating allegory was known in the Dutch wars as the 'Golden Devil'.
centre
The *Sovereign of the Seas*, another of the Pett family's 'great ships', designed by Phineas and built by his son, Peter.
below
Ornamental stern of the seventeenth-century French ship *Soleil Royal*.

When Navies Clashed

The seventeenth century was one of almost unchecked belligerence for the navies of England, France, Holland, Spain and Sweden, and the roll-call of battles reads rather like the fixture list of a small and exclusive football league. In their efforts to find out which ships fired the most effective broadsides, the nations experimented with two and three gun decks, and weighed the advantages of fast ships with limited firepower against those of slower ships with more and heavier guns.

In 1653 the British Admiralty introduced method to what had up till then been a disorderly scene by decreeing that ships were to fight in line ahead. By this tactic the attacking fleet sailed in single file past a chosen point in the enemy's fleet, each ship delivering its broadside and, so it was hoped, through a concentration of fire shattering resistance in that sector.

To determine which vessels were worthy 'ships of the line', all warships were given a rating, from first- to sixth-rate, based on the number of guns carried. Of these, the first three rates were considered powerful enough to fight in the line. The upper ratings were: first rate, more than 90 guns; second rate, more than 80 guns; third rate, more than 50 guns.

below
England versus France at the Battle of Malaga, 1704; from a painting by Isaac Sailmaker.

opposite top
Holland versus Sweden at the Battle of the Sound, 1658; from a painting by Willem van de Velde the Elder.

opposite bottom
Holland versus Spain at the Battle of the Downs, 1639; from a painting by Cornelisz Verbeeck.

top
The Dutch Admiral de Ruyter leads a daring raid along the English River Medway in 1667; from a painting by P. C. van Soest.

above
The Dutch fleet before the Four Days Battle (against England) in 1666.

right
Dutch men of war attack a Spanish fort, and the defenders respond by sending out two galleys and a galleon; from a painting by Adam Willaerts, mid-seventeenth century.

Attack on Naples

This exuberant engraving by Romayn de Hooghe records the thunder and confusion of a Turkish assault on Naples in 1686. Some of the details repay a closer look.

Firstly, in the Mediterranean tradition, the Turkish fleet consists largely of oar-driven galleys. These are aimed bows-on at the city walls, discharging shot from the cannon mounted on their foredecks. The galleys are augmented by smaller bomb craft such as that shown at bottom right. The air is thick with rotund, smoking mortar bombs, and several fires have broken out in the city. In the left foreground a ship's boat, sculled over the stern, touches land and an officer directs the unloading of stores. Beyond them is a gun battery whose crew operate behind a protecting screen of gabions, wickerwork cylinders filled with earth. In the centre of the picture a boarding party is storming the isolated fort while, on land, several battalions in the upper left corner, each consisting of a central 'hedge' of pikemen flanked by its musketeers, are advancing on a flotilla of small ships evidently about to put ashore.

VEROVERING VAN NAPOLI DI ROMAN
ARGOS, TERES CORINTH, et.
NEVENS DE VICTORIE DER S.R. OP DE TURCE

VAN NAPOLI DI ROMANIA

R. de Hooge fecit

Death to All Pirates!

Most notorious of all pirates were the Algerian and Tunisian corsairs, who between the sixteenth and nineteenth centuries plundered every kind of shipping in the Mediterranean from their fast, armed sailing craft. After an attack they withdrew to their heavily fortified home ports along the Barbary coast, a region that stretched westward from Egypt as far as Morocco and was named after the Berber, who were the principal inhabitants. The corsairs also specialized in extracting 'appeasement' levies from the weaker European states, and various expeditions were sent against them, from America as well as Europe. They were finally put to the sword and their empire broken when the French stormed Algiers in 1830.

right
Spanish men of war sink a corsair galley; from a painting by Cornelis Vroom, 1615.

below
Cutlass- and pistol-armed British seamen board an Algerian pirate ship, early nineteenth century.

Guns at Sea

The main types of naval artillery were cannon and mortars. The former were carried in broadsides on one or more decks and usually consisted of heavy smooth-bore muzzle-loaders mounted on wheeled carriages that were run inboard each time the cannon had to be loaded. The cannon had a limited field of fire owing to the gun ports through which they were trained, and the type of fire they gave was of the low-trajectory kind aimed at battering the enemy's 'wooden walls' or at tearing holes in his rigging. Such cannon were the principal weapons of the ships of the line.

By contrast, the mortar offered high-trajectory fire and could fling bombs of considerable weight – up to 200 pounds – into the air to plunge onto enemy ships and onshore defences. The French in 1682 introduced a new type of ship that specialized in this kind of work – the bomb ketch. These beamy vessels had no foremast to impede the departing missiles, and they were specially reinforced to bear the shock of the mortar's recoil.

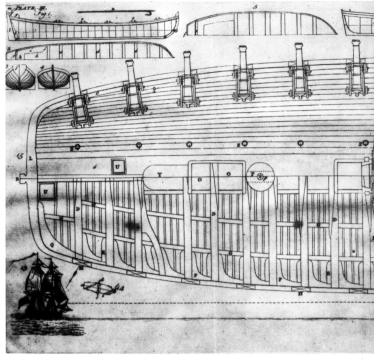

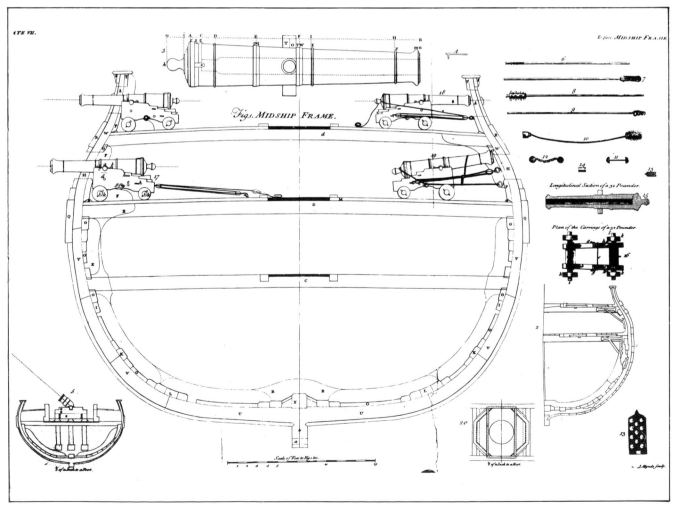

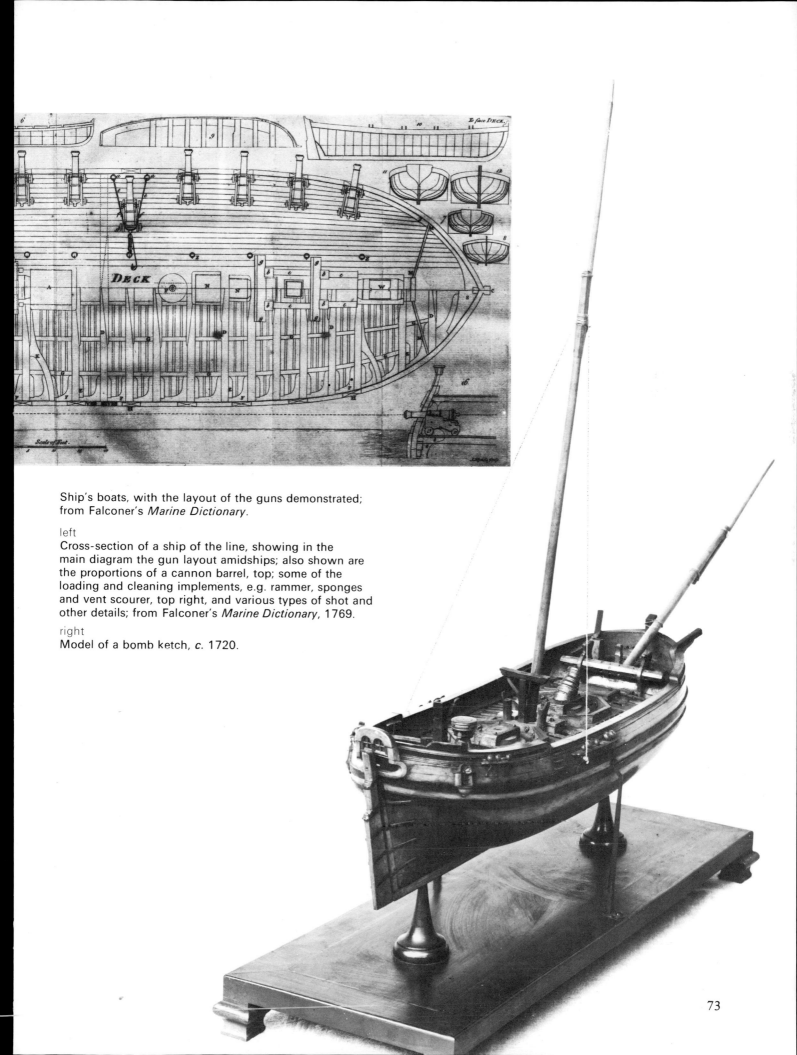

Ship's boats, with the layout of the guns demonstrated;
from Falconer's *Marine Dictionary*.

left
Cross-section of a ship of the line, showing in the
main diagram the gun layout amidships; also shown are
the proportions of a cannon barrel, top; some of the
loading and cleaning implements, e.g. rammer, sponges
and vent scourer, top right, and various types of shot and
other details; from Falconer's *Marine Dictionary*, 1769.

right
Model of a bomb ketch, *c.* 1720.

Britannia Rules!

Under the combined auspices of Queen Anne (reigned 1702–14) and the Duke of Marlborough, Britain enjoyed huge success as a military power, giving rise to feelings of national invincibility that were strengthened as the eighteenth century progressed and have lingered to this day. The most glaring difference between then and now appears to lie in the field of overseas territories, then in the process of being taken, now largely vacated. The illustrations on these pages convey some of the flavour of that grandeur that was special to Britain in the eighteenth century.

What Nobler Prospect can with Eys be seen?
Than such a Powerfull Fleet, and such a Queen?
Each Others Rights they mutually Maintain
She makes them Conquer, and They make Her Reign!

A monumental design in praise of Queen Anne (reigned 1702–14).

above
The taking of Quebec from the Heights of Abraham; James Wolfe's light infantrymen disembark and scramble up the famous 'Woody Precipice' to restore British fortunes in Canada, 1759.

left
'A Prospect of Portsmouth', executed in honour of the then C.-in C., His Majesty's Fleets in the West Indies, 1740.

HMS *Victory*

Nelson's flagship at the Battle of Trafalgar (1805), she was by far the most celebrated ship of her generation. HMS *Victory* was built at Chatham in 1759–65 and twice rebuilt before Trafalgar. She now stands in dry dock at Portsmouth, fully restored to her Trafalgar specification. In her great days she carried 102 guns, of which 30 were 32-pounders, 28 were 24-pounders and the remainder 12-pounders and two 68-pounder carronades, the latter being reserved for close-range duties.

The Victory returning from Trafalgar, by J. M. W. Turner.

right
HMS *Victory*, preserved at Portsmouth.

Scenes From the Napoleonic Wars

The fight against Napoleon Bonaparte lasted from 1792 until 1815. At sea the first major confrontation was the Battle of the First of June 1794, when Lord Howe defeated Admiral Villaret-Joyeuse and captured six French ships. The protracted campaign, which included Nelson's two major battles, at the Nile (1798) and Trafalgar (1805), ended when Napoleon was taken prisoner and sent aboard HMS *Bellerophon* to begin his last exile.

right
Nelson's ships, upper right, advance on the French line at the Battle of the Nile, 1798; from a painting by Nicholas Pocock.

below
Blood and fire on the quarterdeck of the *Queen Charlotte*, Lord Howe's flagship at the Battle of the First of June, 1794.

opposite bottom
The end of an era: Napoleon Bonaparte boards HMS *Bellerophon* on 15 July 1815 to begin the exile from which he never returned.

Chapter 5
Seamanship in 1800

The content of this chapter is largely based on extracts from a guide to practical seamanship written by Darcy Lever and published in 1808 under the title of *The Young Sea Officer's Sheet Anchor*. The book is illustrated throughout with 'a Plate for every Page of Letter Press', and throws valuable light on both the state of knowledge concerning sail and sailing techniques that existed at the beginning of the nineteenth century, and on how this knowledge was passed on to 'the young Gentlemen of the Royal Navy, the Honourable East India Company's Service, and others . . . !

In the section headed 'Sails', Lever introduces his subject with a brisk and straightforward Naming of Parts: 'The Names of the Sails are derived from the Masts to which they are attached: thus the Foresail is named from the Fore Mast, the Mainsail from the Main Mast, the Main Topsail from the Main Top Mast, &c.

'Sails are made of Canvas, the number and strength of which is determined by the size or use of the Sail. The strongest Canvas is called *No. 1*, and it decreases gradually to *No. 8*. Sails are surrounded by a Rope called a *Bolt Rope*; but this is of different denominations according as it is sewn to the Head, Foot or Leech. Thus that at the Head is called the *Head Rope*, that at the Side the *Leech Rope*, and that at the Foot the *Foot Rope*. The Foot Rope is the strongest, the Leech Rope somewhat less, and the Head Rope the least.

'Square Sails are not so called from their Shape; but because they are suspended to Yards, their Heads hanging parallel to their Feet; which distinguishes them from the Staysails or Fore and Aft Sails. They are made of Pieces of Canvas, called *Cloths*, each Piece being two Feet in breadth, having *generally* more of these in the Foot than in the Head. These laying parallel to each other, and perpendicular to the Head, the Breadth of the Sail is diminished by being cut from the lower Corners or Clews (a), Fig. 293, diagonally towards the Head (b). This is called *goring* a Sail. . . .'

'**The Square Sails**, Fig. 291 and 292, are
a   The Fore Sail.
b   The Fore Topsail.
c   The Fore Top Gallant Sail.
d   The Fore Top Gallant Royal.
e   The Fore Studding Sail.
f   The Fore Topmast Studding Sail.
g   The Fore Top-Gallant Studding Sail.
h   The Mainsail.
i   The Main Topsail.
k   The Main Top Gallant Sail.
l   The Main Top Gallant Royal.
m   The Main Topmast Studding Sail.
n   The Main Top Gallant Studding Sail.
o   The Mizen Topsail.
p   The Mizen Top Gallant Sail.
q   The Mizen Top Gallant Royal.
r   The Spritsail.
s   The Spritsail Topsail.

'**The Fore** and **Aft Sails**, are
t   The Jib.
u   The Fore Topmast Staysail.
v   The Fore Staysail.
w   The Main Staysail.
x   The Main Topmast Staysail.
y   The Middle Staysail.
z   The Main Top Gallant Staysail.
aa   The Mizen Staysail.
ab   The Mizen Topmast Staysail.
ac   The Mizen Top Gallant Staysail.
ad   The Driver or Spanker with the Mizen brailed up.

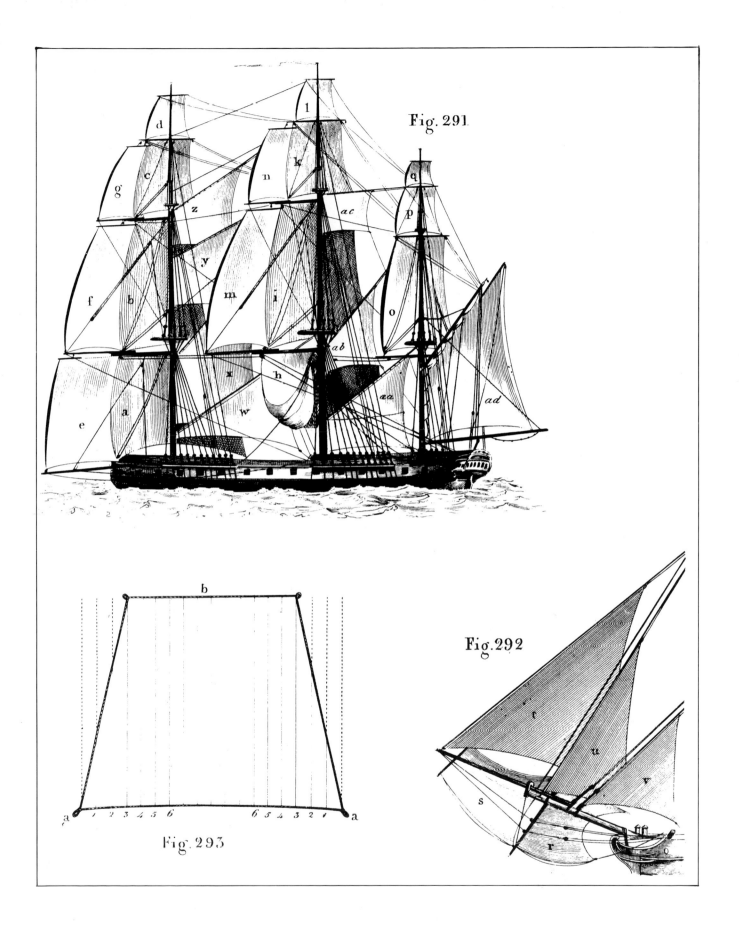

Fig. 291

Fig. 292

Fig. 293

Ropes
and Their Uses

In the opening part of his book, Darcy Lever describes the nature and uses of ropes and rigging: 'The Rigging of a Ship consists of a quantity of Ropes, or Cordage, of various Dimensions, for the support of the Masts and Yards. Those which are fixed and stationary, such as Shrouds, Stays, and Back-stays, are termed *Standing Rigging*; but those which reeve through Blocks, or Sheave-Holes, are denominated *Running Rigging*; such as Halliards, Braces, Clew-lines, Bunt-lines, &c. &c. These are occasionally hauled upon, or let go, for the purpose of working the Ship.

'Ropes are a combination of several Threads of Hemp, twisted together by means of a Wheel in the Rope-Walk. These threads are called Rope-Yarns, and the Size of the Rope in Diameter, will be according to the Number of Yarns contained in it.

'A Proportion of Yarns (covered with Tar) are first twisted together. This is called a Strand; three, or more of which being twisted together, form the Rope: and according to the number of these Strands, it is said to be either *Hawser-laid*, *Shroud-laid*, or *Cable-laid*.

'A Hawser-Laid Rope, Fig. 1.
Is composed of three single Strands, each containing an equal Quantity of Yarns, and is laid right-handed, or what is termed *with the Sun*.

'A Shroud-Laid Rope, Fig. 2.
Consists of four Strands of an Equal Number of Yarns, and is also laid *with the Sun*.

'A Cable-Laid Rope, Fig. 3.
Is divided into nine Strands of an equal Number of Yarns: these *nine* Strands being again laid into *three*, by twisting *three* of the small Strands into *one*. It is laid left-handed or *against the Sun*. . . .'

In addition to describing the three types of rope quoted above, Darcy Lever also deals with two methods of spinning yarn on a winch; these are illustrated in Figs 4 and 5.

top
Ropemakers at work; from the *Encyclopédie Méthodique*, 1787.

right
View through the rigging of a modern sail training ship.

far right
Three types of rope as defined by Lever, also two methods of spinning yarn on a winch.

82

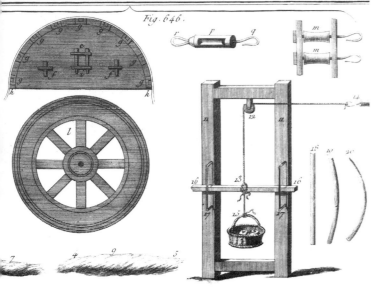

Fig. 644.

Fig. 646.

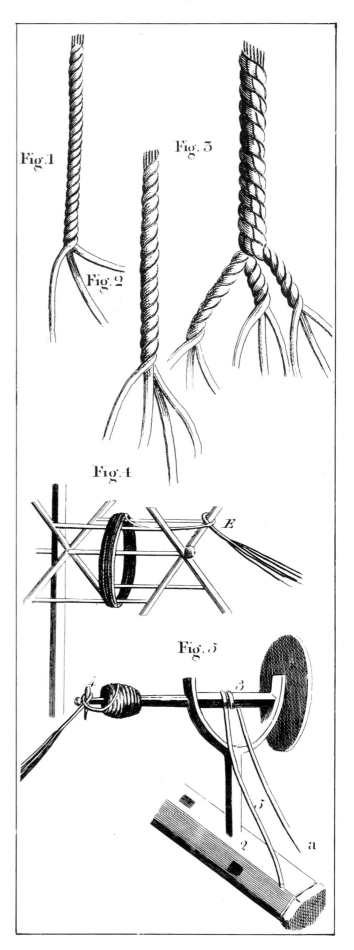

Fig. 1   Fig. 3

Fig. 2

Fig. 4

E

Fig. 5

Knotting

On these pages we reproduce one of the sections in Lever's *Sheet Anchor* devoted to splices and knots and how to make them. (Readers may like to try for themselves.)

'To make the **Cut** or **Bight Splice**, Fig. 19.
Cut a Rope in two, and according to the size of the Collar or Eye you mean to form, lay the end of one Rope upon the standing part of the other, and push the ends through, between the Strands, in the same manner as for the Eye Splice [not shown]. This forms a Collar or Eye, (u) in the bight of the Rope. It is used for Pendents, Jib-Guys, &c.

'To make a **Wall-Knot**, Fig. 21.
Unlay the end of a Rope, Fig. 20, and with the Strand (1) from a Bight, holding it down on the side of the Rope at (2): pass the end of the next (3), round the Strand (1): the end of the Strand (4), round the Strand (3), and through the Bight which was made at first by the Strand (1): haul them rather taught, and the Knot will then appear like Fig. 21.

'To **Crown** this Knot, Fig. 23.
Lay one of the ends over the top of the Knot, Fig. 22, which call the first (a), lay the second (b), over it, and the third (c), over (b), and through the Bight of (a): haul them taught, and the Knot with the Crown will appear like Fig. 23, which is drawn open, in order to render it more clear. This is called a *Single Wall*, and *Single Crown*.

'To **Double Wall** this Knot, Fig. 24.
Take one of the ends of the single Crown, Fig. 23, suppose the end (b), bring it underneath the part of the first walling next to it, and push it up through the same Bight (d): perform this operation with other Strands, pushing them up through two Bights, and the Knot will appear like Fig. 24, having a *double Wall*, and *single Crown*.

'To **Double Crown** the same Knot, Fig. 25.
Lay the Strands by the sides of those in the single Crown, pushing them through the same Bights in the *single* Crown, and down through the *double* Walling: it will then be like Fig. 25, viz. *single* walled, *single* crowned, *double* walled, and *double* crowned. This is sometimes called a Tack Knot, and is also used for Topsail Sheets. The first walling must always be made *against* the lay of the Rope: the parts will then lay fair for the double crown; so that if Figure 20 had been a hawser-laid Rope, or *with the Sun*, the Strands (1, 3, 4) would have been passed the contrary way. The ends are scraped down, tapered, marled, and served with spun-yarn.

'**Mathew Walker's Knot**, Fig. 27,
is made by separating the Strands of a Rope, Fig. 26, taking the end (1) round the rope, and through its own Bight: the end (2) underneath, through the Bight of the first, and through its own Bight, and the end (3) underneath, through the Bights of the Strands (1 and 2), and through its own Bight. Haul them taught, and they form the Knot Fig. 27. The ends are cut off. This is a handsome Knot for the end of a Laniard.

'N.B. The Knots are in general drawn very slack and open, that the parts may be more plainly demonstrated: on which account they have not so neat an appearance in the plates, as when they are hauled taught. More bights and turns are also shewn in the drawings, than can be seen at one view in the Knots, without turning them backwards and forwards.'

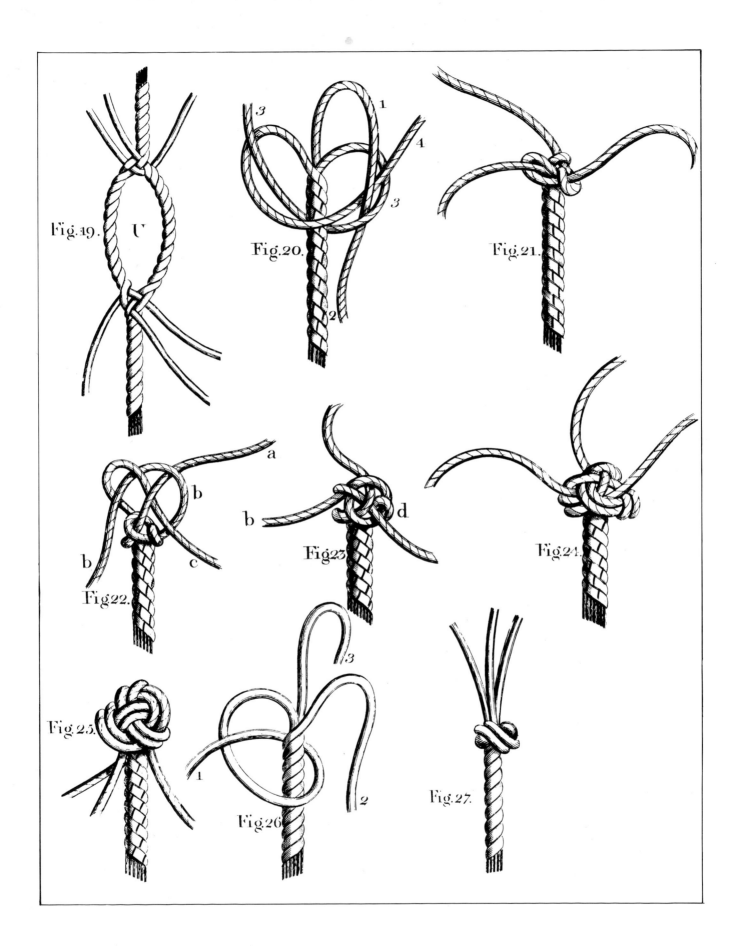

Fig.19. U

Fig.20.

Fig.21.

Fig22.

Fig23.

Fig.24.

Fig.25.

Fig26.

Fig.27.

Bending the Foresail

In the illustration below, Figs 301–307 describe the process known as bending the foresail, i.e. hauling it up to the yard and making it fast. This operation involved eight men who perched along the yard and pulled the sail up by the yard-ropes (p) and the bunt-lines (q). Lever writes: 'The Head of the Sail is then hauled well upon the Yard; the *long* legs of the Rope-bands (k), being *before* the Sail, are taken over and under the Yard with a round Turn; and the *short* ones (h) being brought up *abaft* it, they are made fast by a Reef-knot. . . .'

The clippers *Taeping* (left) and *Ariel* at the climax of their 99-day race from Foochow to London in 1866.

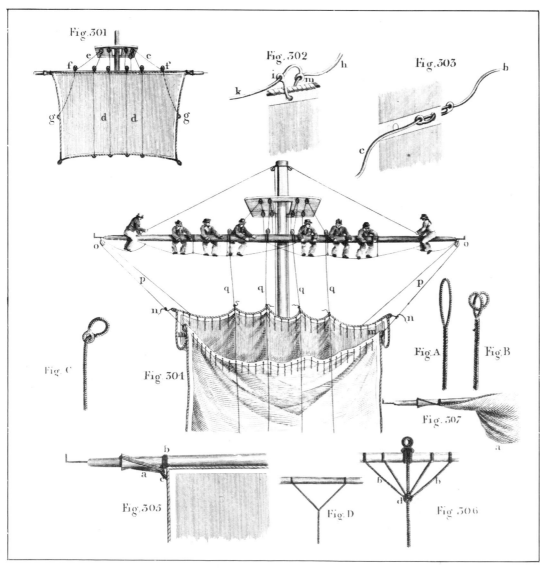

Tacking

Lever now demonstrates the principles of tacking by showing 'the method formerly practised'. He then analyses this method and criticizes it on five grounds at some length before he proposes an alternative method of 'expeditious' tacking. Although it is not appropriate here to explore Lever's highly technical arguments, the illustrations themselves are interesting in that they show something rarely seen – the manoeuvres of a full-rigged ship explained in the form of a step-by-step diagram.

The four stages show the ship on the starboard tack (Fig. 399) with the wind at ENE; she will shortly be put about to stand on the larboard (port) tack. The compass diagram (Fig. 403) shows the direction of the ship at each step of the manoeuvre. Next (Fig. 400) she is brought round gradually eastward until her head is within three points of the wind. The wind now blows on the extremities of the after sails and is seen to make them shake. In Fig. 401 the ship is brought head to wind and then (Fig. 402) more rudder is used to face her SE on the larboard tack.

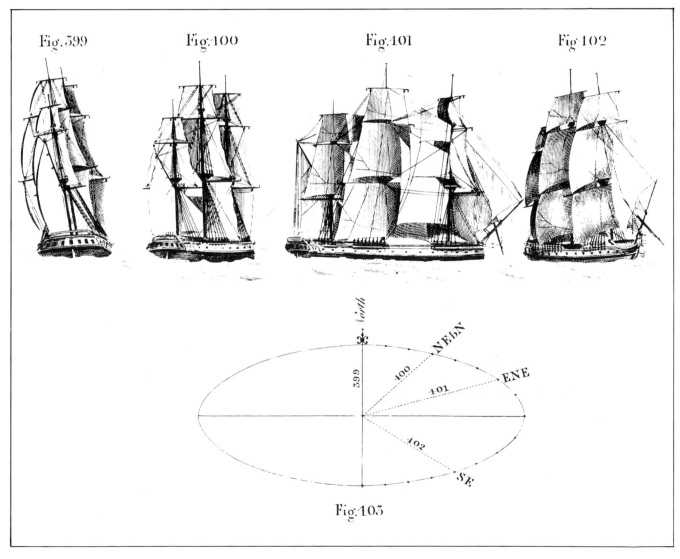

Fig. 399 Fig. 400 Fig. 401 Fig. 402

Fig. 403

Sounding

Here Lever discusses how to take soundings, to determine depth, etc. 'When Soundings are tried for, it is done by the deep Sea Lead, on the Bottom of which is put a Composition of Tallow: this is called *arming* the Lead: so that when it touches the Ground, it brings up some of that substance which lies on the Surface, such as Sand, Corral, Shells, Oaze [ooze = mud, slime, formerly also seaweed], &c. and by these (from repeated trials being made and marked in the Charts), the bearings of certain Headlands, Rocks, Buoys, Sands, &c. are generally known.

'If a Ship be going free with a light Breeze, Soundings may be got by passing the Lead to windward from the Quarter along the Waist to the Cat-head; or if that be not sufficient, a Hand is sent out to the Spritsail Yard Arm (a), Fig. 506; and another (carrying the Bight of the Line) to the Jib Boom End (b). The Man (a), heaves the Lead from him, and the Man (b), swings it forward: as the Ship advances, the Line being veered away from a Reel, a Hand in the Mizen Chains (d), gets the Soundings. The Bight of the Line is then put into a small snatch Block made fast to the Mizen Shrouds, hauled in, and reeled up.'

Fig. 506 shows the crew positions for taking soundings in a light breeze.

The 'Hand in the Mizen Chains' — positioned at (d) in the diagram — takes the soundings; from a contemporary painting.

Fig. 506

Chapter 6
Sail in the age of Steam

The final phase of the sailing ship was to be its most glorious. Like the massed galleys and galleasses at Lepanto in 1571, the sailing ship had already been technologically surpassed by the time she reached her greatest heights of refinement. After Lepanto the gunned sailing ship had taken over; by the end of the nineteenth century the focus of power at sea had in most places been transferred to the engine room. Both newcomers, the galleon and the steamship, nevertheless required long settling-in periods: thus combinations of galley and galleass lived on in the Mediterranean fleets for 150 years or so, while the sailing ship is with us still, even though its duties are for the most part limited and localized.

For a long while, until the beginning of the twentieth century at least, sail and steam lived more or less as equals. Steam began to arrive in the decade after William Symington, a Scotsman, in 1801 unveiled the *Charlotte Dundas*, a Clyde canal tug. At first the new method of propulsion was unreliable and uneconomic, and could not compete over long distances with the powerful East Indiamen. Except among the most radical of the pioneering ships, steam power provided at best an auxiliary source. Gradually, though, the power ship acquired greater capabilities. In the early 1840s a new firm, the British and North American Royal Mail Steam Packet Company, inaugurated a regular monthly transatlantic service with a fleet of paddle-wheelers. The 1840s was also the decade of the screw propeller, patented by Captain Ericsson, a Swedish engineer; and by 1845 Brunel's *Great Britain* had become the first screw-propelled ship to cross the Atlantic.

It is nevertheless strange that all these industrial wonders should be achieved *ahead of* the sailing ship's greatest phase – the era of the racing clipper. In this chapter we look at how these and other vessels proved that the nineteenth-century sailing ship was far from being the aquatic dinosaur that some marine inventors may have wished.

The SS *Europe*; a predecessor of the clipper ship, she was built in New York in 1833 and sailed with the Black Ball Line, which in 1816 had opened a service between New York and Liverpool.

A waterfront scene in nineteenth-century Canton, showing a colourful parade of junks, yachts and a paddle-wheeler.

below
The launch of the *Demologos* in New York, 1814; she was a pioneering double-keeled steam warship designed (belatedly, as it turned out) to challenge the Royal Navy's supremacy in the War of 1812.

The Full-Rigged Ship

From among the proliferation of ship types that sailed the world in the nineteenth century, it may be helpful to separate, firstly, a handful of those generally thought to be the most important by virtue of their size and the numbers of sails that they carried. At the head of any such list must come the full-rigged ship. She had at least three principal masts, all of them square-rigged, and each bearing five or more sails. On the mainmast these were called the mainsail, main lower topsail, main upper topsail, main topgallant and main royal. Above these there might be a main skysail. Full-rigged ships also carried three to four sails forward of the foremast: reading foreward, these were the fore staysail, fore topmast staysail, jib and flying jib.

The full-rigged ships undertook all kinds of duties. There were emigrant ships, taking people from Britain and Europe to new lives in the USA and Australia, tea and wool clippers and Blackwall frigates, named after the London yard where they were built. In the early part of the century these ships were made of wood; later they were built with stronger hulls of first iron, then steel. Perhaps the grandest of all the full-riggers was the 5,080-ton German ship *Preussen*: she was launched in 1902 and had five masts carrying 47 sails and a total of 59,000 square feet of canvas.

below
The SS *Torrens* (1875) which worked the Australian trade and for a time had as her mate the novelist Joseph Conrad.

right
A photograph of the full-rigger *Atlas*.

The Clippers

The clippers, that most dramatic of the sailing breed, were of a multiplicity of types and rigs. An early version was the three-masted Baltimore clipper: later came Blackwall frigates, tall barques, schooners and full-rigged ships. One factor, though, singles out the archetypal clipper – its long, narrow, racing lines. For the clippers depended on speed above all else, even cargo capacity, for their success. Literally, they 'clipped' the wind. If a clipper was to be profitable, it had to be faster than its competitors, which by the 1850s included power-ships of increasing reliability and greater capacity.

A major event that spurred clipper development came in 1849 when the British Navigation Acts were repealed, so opening up a previously closed-shop trade to all-comers. The Americans were quick to assert their interest, and the efficiency of their merchantmen was soon a byword. The year 1849 was also the year of the California gold rush, when it seemed there were never enough ships to carry gold-crazed speculators to San Francisco. Meanwhile the Far East was fountainhead to a bustling tea trade as well as a less creditable traffic in opium; and at the same time the Australian wool trade was expanding. Everything in fact conspired to make the dashing clipper the ideal vessel for the times – so long as it could keep up its own searing pace . . . 97 days from Hong Kong to London; Melbourne to Liverpool in 63 days; Newcastle, New South Wales to Shanghai in 28 days; Foochow to Gravesend, against the monsoon, in 91 days; Boston Light to Liverpool in 13 days 19½ hours; 436 miles in a day's run. The mood of the competitors was at times closer to hysteria than commercial enthusiasm, and no ships were driven harder than the clippers; many were commanded by rampaging captains and sadistic mates, suitably nicknamed Bully This and Bully That.

In the end it was the desperate search for extra speed that undermined the clippers' position and hastened their demise. To achieve a faster shape, their lines were progressively reduced until they had become overbred for their function: eventually too narrow to carry enough wool or tea for the prices their owners could get, they found their market deserting them. There was no scope for a comeback, the march of steam was irreversible. And so the slender 'China birds', the 'ghosters', as they had been known in their prime, slid away to extinction.

These illustrations are all from paintings by the British marine artist J. Spurling.

below
Sovereign of the Seas, a 2,421-ton American clipper built in Boston by Donald McKay, one of the great shipbuilders of the age.

opposite top
The *Cutty Sark*, possibly the most famous of the British clippers; she now lies at Greenwich in dry dock.

opposite bottom
The *Mount Stewart*, a wool ship that worked in the Australian trade.

opposite top
The *James Baines*, built in Boston by Donald McKay in 1854 and named after the Liverpool shipowner who ordered her and three other clippers from McKay's yard.

opposite bottom
The *Flying Cloud*; another distinguished McKay clipper ship, she worked the San Francisco run.

above
Donald McKay's *Glory of the Seas* is about to be launched, in 1869; McKay himself stands before her (in top hat).

The clipper ship *Lahloo,* 1867.

Barques and Barquentines

One of the classic sailing types was the barque, first developed in the eighteenth century. These were three-, four- or sometimes five-masted ships. The staple three-masted type was square-rigged on fore- and mainmast, while the mizzen carried a gaff and boomsail; its function was that of the medium-sized trader and it was found on both sides of the Atlantic.

The need for at least one more mast came about as the demands made on transport ships increased. Overseas trade was booming and shipowners looked about for ways of stepping up capacity. At the same time, in the 1870s, the narrow clippers were no longer such a good cargo-carrying proposition, for all their speed. One answer was to scale up the barque by giving her three square-rigged masts and a fourth that was a fore-and-aft jigger. After the 1880s barques were also equipped with steel hulls that could embrace larger cargoes and were better able to withstand the stresses of a transatlantic buffeting. Their only drawback was that the iron wire rigging and steel masts and spars were prone to snap; and when they did, they needed specialized equipment to repair them that an ordinary crew could not provide in the course of a voyage.

A more economical ship was devised on the West Coast of North America, the barquentine. She was square-rigged on her foremast only, the remainder being of the fore-and-aft type. This possibly odd-looking hybrid in fact made a safe and efficient cargo carrier, and in time a number of square-riggers were converted to this design.

left
The four-masted barque *Routenburn*, built at Greenock in 1881; her type was square-rigged on three masts with a fore-and-aft rig on the last, known as the jigger.

bottom
The hard life at sea; from *Manual Labour*, by A. R. Thompson.

Brigs

The brig was a less grand type than ships of the barque/barquentine family. Her rig – two square-rigged masts with a gaff and boomsail set from the lower part of the mainmast – suited the trader of some 100 feet in length overall, designed to carry, for example, coal along the North Sea coast of England. A related type was the brigantine, also known in North America as the half brig or hermaphrodite brig. These had two masts with square sails on the foremast and a fore-and-aft sail on the mainmast.

The *Vencateswaraloo*, a brig that still works today among the islands of the Indian Ocean.

right
An English trading brig off Bristol, 1838; from a painting by Joseph Walter.

Schooners

Originally a two-masted vessel rigged mostly with fore-and-aft sails, the schooner developed out of Dutch and British rigs of the yacht type in the early part of the eighteenth century. A hundred years later there emerged the classic schooner type that was reproduced in great numbers and in all kinds of sizes on both sides of the Atlantic. The Americans built more schooners than any other nation, and their versions were typically fore-and-aft rigged with two or more masts. British schooners differed somewhat in that many of them carried square sails on the fore topmast. The smaller schooners worked as coastal cargo carriers while the enlarged types – massive ships with, usually, four or five masts – served as deep-sea carriers and in specialized work such as the Newfoundland cod-fishing industry. Largest of all the schooners was the *Thomas W. Lawson*, a gigantic steel-hulled seven-master of more than 5,000 tons, launched in 1902 and lost in the Scilly Isles in 1907 after a brief but profitable career. Shipowners, in the USA in particular, liked the big schooners because they beat nearly all their rivals handsomely for capacity and also because they could be operated by a small crew – only 16 men, for instance, being needed to handle the *Lawson*. These were factors that helped to keep the schooner in business in the North Atlantic until the 1930s.

A parade of nineteenth-century schooners:
below
The two-masted *Franc Miner*, built in 1885.
opposite top
The only one of her kind – the giant seven-master *Thomas W. Lawson* (1902), seen here in a model version.
opposite bottom
The *Inca*, a five-masted ship built in 1896 for the Pacific trade.

Two ships that express the twin concerns of merchant sail in the nineteenth century — speed and bulk:

above
The sturdy five-masted barquentine *Annie Comyn*.

right
The lean clipper ship *Hurricane*.

Ships of War

Naval strategists were happier than merchant ship-owners to discard sail as soon as the new marine engines of the Industrial Revolution had proved themselves. No longer, ran their thinking, need warships risk being becalmed; they would also be strategically more mobile, as well as tactically handier in a fight. Sail nevertheless persisted until well after the Crimean War (1853–56), though increasingly in an auxiliary capacity. The mid-century was also the period that saw the old 'wooden walls' superseded by, first of all, wooden ships protected by iron cladding, and soon afterwards by iron- and steel-hulled vessels.

The Royal Navy had several steam tugs in operation by the 1820s. And although paddle-driven fighting ships were not a success – the paddles were vulnerable to enemy fire and their presence prohibited the carrying of guns amidships – a lasting solution to the problem of propulsion was near at hand. This was the screw propeller, first introduced in a capital ship in 1850. By 1858 the navies of France and Britain both had 38 ships fitted with auxiliary screw power, and more quickly followed.

Advances in shell technology at this time compelled the naval authorities also to seek better protection for their ships; the days of wood were numbered. Iron was at first too brittle under fire: in 1840 the sides of a test ship, the *Ruby*, had shattered and sent lethal

below
La Gloire; first of a new type, the iron-protected frigate, she was laid down in 1858.

opposite bottom
HMS *Warrior*, the world's first iron warship, launched in 1860.

splinters flying round her interior. But the quality of iron improved and in 1858 the French engineer Dupuy de Lôme produced *La Gloire*, a wooden-hulled two-decker whose exterior was armoured with more effective iron plates. Two years later the British introduced the *Warrior*, a 9,210-ton armoured frigate built entirely of iron.

The industrialization of the world's navies continued at an impressive pace. Sails were still carried, but the screw propeller was clearly the device of the future. Meanwhile, the principle of the long-established broadside was being challenged by a new system of mounting guns in turrets that gave all-round fire. The guns themselves were getting bigger and heavier, too, and by the late 1860s it was apparent that their weight, added to that of the armoured hull, made progress under sail a dangerously slow and unseaworthy affair. The approaching end of 4,000 years of sail in war was confirmed in 1871 when HMS *Devastation* was launched. She was the first mastless battleship, and she had a steaming radius of 4,700 miles. For the many reactionary voices that cried doom when they heard of this coal-only monster, there was little consolation. Sails were preserved on cruisers and lighter ships until the 1880s, but by then their function was merely to conserve coal stocks. The fighting days of sail were irreversibly done.

An impression of the Battle of Lissa, fought in 1866 and remembered as marking the untimely return of the near-antique ram to the 'modern' warship. In this battle the Austrian battleship *Ferdinand Max* successfully rammed and sank the Italian battleship *Re d'Italia*. For some years afterwards the bows of European warships sprouted rams, until it became clear that the ram was a thoroughly outmoded weapon in an age of high manoeuvrability. Rams then vanished forever.

Goodbye England

To help the thousands of people determined to leave Britian for a new life in America or Australia, that most resourceful and level-headed of English writers, William Cobbett, in 1829 produced an *Emigrant's Guide*. It is a storehouse of practical information laced with personal insights. Discussing the 'sort of Ship to go in', Cobbett prefers to ignore the merits of the ships themselves; instead he is much more concerned about the quality of the captains, which leads him to make some interesting national distinctions. He begins firmly:

'The ship will be no other than an *American* one, if you wish for a *quick* and a *safe* passage. The Americans sail *faster* than others, owing to the greater *skill* and greater *vigilance* of the captains, and to their great sobriety and the wise rules that they observe with regard to their men. They carry *more sail* than other ships; because the captain is everlastingly looking out. I have crossed the Atlantic three times in American ships, once in an English merchant ship, once in a king's ship, and once in a king's packet; and I declare, that the superiority of the Americans is decided, and so decided, that, if I were going to cross again, nothing should prevail on me to go on board of any ship but an American one. I never knew an American captain *take off his clothes to go to bed, during the whole voyage*; and I never knew any other who did not do it. The consequence of this great watchfulness is, that, advantage is taken of every puff of wind, while the risk from the squalls and sudden gusts is, in a great measure, obviated. A lazy captain, or one that gets drunk over night, does one of two things: keeps out too much sail, and thereby risks the ship, or, in order to avoid danger in this way, keeps out much less than might be carried, and thus the ship is retarded in her progress.'

As for the quality of life on board, Cobbett recommends his readers to take a cabin, especially if there are women and children in the party, rather than going steerage. His book contains ample evidence of the stifling quarters, the misery, disease and death suffered by travellers in steerage. 'If you know of any coming here,' wrote one émigré from New York, 'tell them never to come where the vessel is so full; for we was shut down in darkness for a fortnight, till so many died; then the hatch was opened.'

On a more cheerful note Cobbett gives sound advice on food and drink for the voyage. 'In the cabin, the provisions are found by the Captain, and that is by far the best way; but, in the steerage, it is best to take your own provisions . . . Flour, rice, ginger, candles, grots, salt, pepper, vinegar, port wine . . . dried ham, other bacon, potatoes, butter, sugar, tea, coffee. You should take some biscuits, and perhaps three or four times as much as you want, for fear of a long voyage, and consequent famine . . . I would add, some fresh eggs, well packed in bran or salt; I do not recollect anything else, except a bottle of brandy for the steerage passenger, and a gallon of brandy for the cabin passenger, to be judiciously administered in *bribes* to the *black cook*. He would bid you toss your money into the sea; but he will suck down your brandy; and you will get many a nice thing prepared by him, which you would never get, if it were not for that brandy.'

Assuredly, the way of the emigrant in the first half of the century was beset with all kinds of traps. Conditions in the sailing ships did improve considerably, however, and in time doctors began to recommend a cabin class passage under sail – in preference to steam – as being the most restful and desirable way to preface a new life in a far-off country. The photograph of life on board the *Macquarie* perhaps illustrates what the doctors had in mind.

Ford Maddox Brown's painting, *The Last of England*, 1855. This work was inspired by the departure for Australia of a fellow artist, Thomas Woolner, and his wife. Brown himself saw the Woolners take their leave, and later he wrote of his painting: 'This picture . . . treats of the great emigration movement, which attained its culminating point in 1852. The educated are bound to their country by closer ties than the illiterate whose chief consideration is food and physical comfort. I have, therefore, in order to present the parting scene in its fullest tragic development, singled out a couple from the middle classes, high enough, through education and refinement, to appreciate all they are now giving up, and yet dignified enough to put up with the discomforts and humiliations incident to a vessel "all one class". The husband broods bitterly over blighted hopes. . . .'

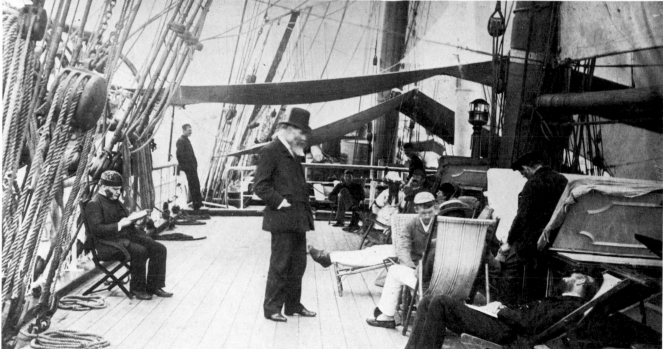

top
The *Macquarie*, a superior passenger ship well known in the Australian trade; from a painting by J. Spurling.

above
On the poop deck of the *Macquarie*; the photograph shows first-class passengers relaxing in gentle, warm weather.

The Ships of E. W. Cooke

Edward William Cooke (1811–81), the son of a well-established engraver, George Cooke, began work at an early age in his father's studio in Barnes, near London, together with apprentices that included Thomas Shotter Boys, the watercolourist and lithographer. There he developed a precocious talent for drawing, and contributed among other works to Loddige's *Botanical Cabinet* (1818–33), for which his father had been commissioned to engrave the plates.

E. W. Cooke was soon to find a special sympathy for marine subjects, and he spent long hours by the river in London and travelled also to ports on the east and south coasts of England, from Great Yarmouth round to Portsmouth, sketching and recording with a light yet craftsmanlike touch the activities on the beaches and wharfsides. In 1829, when he was only 18, a collection of his drawings was published under the title *Sixty-five Plates of Shipping and Craft*. On some of the pages that follow we reproduce a number of these good-humoured, small-scale works.

Cooke evidently found great pleasure in working with naturally picturesque subjects, and we in turn can derive a similar pleasure from looking at the results. The ships appear to have been accurately drawn; Cooke was probably conscientious in this respect, and he is known to have made use of a recent invention, the Graphic Telescope, to ensure that his perspectives were correct. His scenes retain much of the atmosphere of life among coastal ships and their sailors in the late 1820s – the washing strung up on the prison hulk, the busy press of carts and men at the quayside in Yarmouth, the crew of the collier aloft on the mainmast – these are moments from times past that were seldom recorded, and in them lies much of the value of E. W. Cooke's collection.

In the centre of this frieze-like arrangement is the Gravesend steam packet *Rapid* with, astern in the picture, a Thames sailing barge and, on her starboard bow, a collier brig.

above
Dutch galliots, one of the many types of trading vessel to be found in the North Sea ports in the early nineteenth century.

right
A Prussian snow, a two-masted brig-type coastal trader, rests at her moorings.

Two paintings by a marine master, J. M. W. Turner.
(Incidentally, Turner contributed a number of drawings to
Cooke's *Picturesque Views of the Southern Coast of
England*, published by George Cooke, E. W.'s father.)

above
*Calais Pier — French fishermen preparing for sea, the
English packet arriving.* This detail catches much of the
atmosphere, including the discomforts, of life in and out
of small Channel craft in the mid-nineteenth century.

right
Sun rising through vapour; the craft in the foreground
are of the same rig as the long-lived Thames sailing
barge.

More ships by E. W. Cooke:

above
A collier discharges some of its load into a barge.

below
Hay boats, one with her mast lowered, make gentle
progress in flat water.

Convicts arrive with a military escort at their new
temporary home, a decaying prison ship at anchor in
Portsmouth harbour. It was in such hulks that prisoners
were detained while they waited to be deported to
Australia.

Ships that survived the first harsh winds of the
Industrial Revolution:

above
A single-masted Norfolk wherry; with her long gaff and
no boom, she was designed for the quiet inland
waterways of low-lying East Anglia.

left
The steel-hulled, four-masted barque *Carradale*.

right
Now a training ship – the Baltic ketch *Seute Deern*.

Fishing Types

Fishing under sail had a strongly local flavour, each stretch of coast preferring its own style of boat, rig and life-long routine. Until the steam trawler took over towards the end of the nineteenth century, the lug-rigged vessel was the most commonly found in Britain; boats carrying it were usually two-masted and, as was common to all fishing craft, needed large crews to man the heavy nets. Single-masted smacks of various rigs were favoured in many parts, but after the 1870s they were to some extent superseded by two-masted vessels of the yawl and ketch type, such as those of the Scarborough herring fleet illustrated overleaf.

Among fishermen the sailing vessel died hard. Partly because their small, inbred communities were made up of poor men, and partly because these men were disinclined to change the way they lived, it was there, perhaps, that the spirit of the working sailing ship had penetrated most deeply, and there that it survived longest of all.

Coastal fishing types and traders portrayed by E. W. Cooke:

below
A schooner and smack lying at Fresh Wharf, London Bridge.

opposite top
A lugger beached near the Blockade Station, Brighton.

opposite bottom
A Yarmouth herring boat, a lugger, unloads her catch at the quayside.

below
The herring fleet at Scarborough, photographed in 1897.

bottom
The yawl *Bona* in 1903.

right
Last memories of sail . . . a Thames sailing barge
follows a full-rigged ship out to sea.

List of Books Consulted

Archibald, E. H. H., *The Metal Fighting Ship in the Royal Navy 1860–1970* (Blandford, London, 1971).

Bassett-Lowke, W. J. and Holland, George, *Ships and Men* (Harrap, London, 1946).

Brain, Robert, *Into the Primitive Environment* (Philip, London, 1972).

Brophy, Patrick, *Sailing Ships* (Hamlyn, London and Galahad Books, New York, 1974).

Cobbett, William, *The Emigrant's Guide* (London, 1829).

Cooke, E. W., *Sixty-five Plates of Shipping and Craft* (London, 1829).

Goldsmith-Carter, George, *Sailing Ships & Sailing Craft* (Hamlyn, London and Sun Books, Melbourne, 1969).

Green, Peter, *The Year of Salamis, 480–479 BC* (Weidenfeld & Nicolson, London, 1970).

Greenhill, Basil, *James Cook: The Opening of the Pacific* (HMSO, London, 1970).

Greenhill, Basil and Giffard, Ann, *The Merchant Sailing Ship* (David & Charles, Newton Abbot, 1970).

Landström, Björn, *Sailing Ships* (Allen & Unwin, London, 1969).

Lever, Darcy, *The Young Sea Officer's Sheet Anchor* (Leeds, 1808).

Lubbock, B., *Sail, Romances of the Clipper Ships* (London, 1927).

Macintyre, Captain Donald (ed.), *The Adventure of Sail 1520–1914* (Elek, London, 1970).

Moore, Sir Alan, Bt, *Sailing Ships of War 1800–1860* (Halton & Truscott Smith, London and Milton, Balch & Co., New York, 1926).

Ormond, Richard, *The Pre-Raphaelites and their Circle* (Birmingham Museum and Art Gallery, 1965).

Padfield, Peter, *Guns at Sea* (Evelyn, London, 1973).

Sheppard, E. W., *A Visual History of Modern Britain – War* (Studio Vista, London, 1967).

Shepperson, Wilbur S., *British Emigration to North America* (Blackwell, Oxford, 1957).

Swinburne, H. L., *The Royal Navy* (A. & C. Black, London, 1907).

Warner, Oliver, *Great Battle Fleets* (Hamlyn, London, 1973).

Warner, Oliver, *Great Sea Battles* (Spring Books, London, 1968).

Yadin, Yigael, *The Art of Warfare in Biblical Lands* (Weidenfeld & Nicolson, London, 1963).

Bisected in retirement . . . old boats converted to make rope houses on Brighton beach, 1830; drawn and etched by E. W. Cooke.

Acknowledgments

Photographs

Bodleian Library Oxford (Publication 161C) 14–15; British Museum, London 29 bottom, 31 right, 37, 39 top right, 58 left, 68–69; Paul Elek Ltd, London 47, 67 bottom, 90, 106 left, 118 bottom; Mary Evans Picture Library, London 50 left; Photographie Giraudon, Paris 24, 25 left, 42 bottom, 63, 108; Librairie Hachette, Paris 30–31; Hamlyn Group – John Webb 43 bottom, 110, 115 bottom; Hamlyn Group Picture Library 10 bottom, 17 top, 18–19 top, 21 bottom, 22, 23 top, 23 bottom, 25 right, 26, 27 top, 27 bottom, 34–35, 38–39, 43 top, 46 top, 46 bottom, 50–51 bottom, 54, 55 top, 58–59, 62, 66–67 top, 70–71, 78–79 top, 81, 83 right, 85, 86 bottom, 86–87 top, 87 bottom, 88, 91 top, 94, 95 top, 95 bottom, 98–99, 103, 111 top, 112 top, 112 bottom, 113, 116 top, 117 top, 116–117 bottom, 120, 121 top, 121 bottom, 125; A. F. Kersting, London 77; Larousse, Paris 79 bottom; Mansell Collection, London 17 bottom, 74 left; Mariners Museum, Newport News, Virginia 33, 93; Mas, Barcelona 21 top, 55 bottom; Mr and Mrs Paul Mellon 76; National Army Museum, London 74–75 top; National Gallery, London 114–115; National Maritime Museum, London 7, 28, 39 bottom right, 40 top, 40 bottom, 44–45, 45 top, 52, 53 top, 64, 65 bottom, 70 left, 74–75 bottom, 78 bottom, 89, 91 bottom, 96 bottom, 100 top, 101 top, 105 bottom, 109 top, 109 bottom, 111 bottom, 118 top, 122 top; Nederlandsch Historisch Scheepvaart

Sources of Illustrations